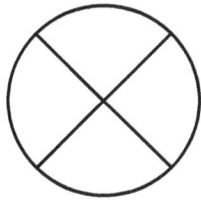  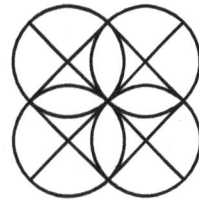

SHOWINGUPBOOK.COM

Lorian Press, LLC
Traverse City | Michigan

LORIANPRESS.COM

SHOWING UP

PRACTICES FOR A SPIRITED LIFE

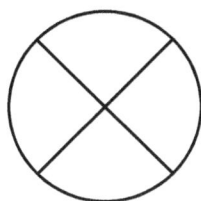

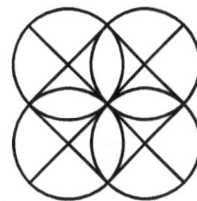

FREYA SECREST

WITH LYRA ZIEGLER

Showing Up | Practices For A Spirited Life

ISBN: 978-0-936878-98-0
Published by Lorian Press, LLC
Traverse City, Michigan
Printed in the United States of America

First Edition

To Lyra and Brendan for your encouragement to get to the point.

POLISH YOUR PATIENCE.

SCULPT THE SACRED OUT OF YOUR DAY.

ELECTRIFY HORIZONTAL SPIRITUALITY.

LEAN INTO HUMILITY.

WEAVE KINDNESS.

MAKE SPACE FOR THOSE THAT ANNOY YOU.

SHARE YOUR MISTAKES.

STACK YOUR GRATITUDE.

JUICE UP YOUR JOY.

AMAZE YOUR BED BY MAKING IT.

TICKLE TABOOS.

FALL INTO FREEDOM.

DESIGN FOR CONNECTION.

COMPLIMENT THE AWKWARD.

INTRODUCE YOUR CELL PHONE TO A TREE.

WATER YOUR PARTNERSHIPS.

DANCE WITH YOUR EDGE.

POSITION YOURSELF FOR PASSION.

EMBRACE YOUR ARTISTRY.

SAY NO TO NUMBNESS.

AIR OUT YOUR ASSUMPTIONS.

COMMIT TO ALIVENESS.

ACTIVATE PRESENCE.

GIFT YOUR PASSION.

CUDDLE UP TO FEAR.

FOSTER CONNECTION.

ACKNOWLEDGEMENTS

This book has evolved through the shared fellowship of a collective of explorers I am honored to call colleagues, friends and family.

David Spangler, whose generosity of spirit always inspires me.

Dorothy Maclean, whose courage to share her experience of God helps me give voice to my own.

Jeremy Berg, whose love, creativity and partnership helps me show up to new parts of myself. I give you my hand in love—and use the other to hold on to my hat.

Lewis, Sarah, Sophia, LR and KFH, who inspire me to get up early.

Drena Griffith, whose editing artistry helped this book settle into place.

Rue Hass, Julia Spangler, Mary Inglis, Adele Napier, Judy McAllister, James Tousignant, Susan Sherman, Tim Hass, Suzanne Fageol, Ruth Chaffee and Elizabeth Fowler who are valued creative and collaborative partners.

TABLE OF CONTENTS

PARTICULARITY

⊗ ## Relationship
MAKE SPACE FOR THOSE THAT ANNOY YOU
WATER YOUR PARTNERSHIPS
SHARE YOUR MISTAKES
TICKLE TABOOS
INTRODUCE YOUR CELL PHONE TO A TREE
DESIGN FOR CONNECTION

⊛ ## Co-Creation
FOSTER CONNECTION
WEAVE KINDNESS
GIFT YOUR PASSION
ELECTRIFY HORIZONTAL SPIRITUALITY
FALL INTO FREEDOM
DANCE WITH YOUR EDGE

POSSIBILITY

SCULPT THE SACRED OUT OF YOUR DAY

PREFACE

There was a moment in my life that sticks out very vividly in my memory. I had just returned from several years residency at the Findhorn Foundation, a spiritual community in northern Scotland where a spiritual focus is woven into every activity of community life. It was an ordinary day; I was riding with a friend and we were merging onto Highway 101 outside of San Francisco. I was thinking about how to continue to deepen my spiritual life in my new urban environment when I suddenly woke up to the fact that the Sacred was not limited to a specific place or set of activities. If it could be found in northern Scotland, it could also be present anywhere, as a seed in everything. In that moment on the highway I decided to look for, be present to, and engage fully with the Sacred wherever and however it shaped itself. That moment was my call to action, everyday spirited action. It was a call to engage my spiritual practice in a broader way.

Many of the larger values and goals I hold for my life—Peace, Love, Freedom, Happiness—sometimes seem far outside my immediate control. I can lose the thread, the step-by-step connection between my everyday actions and these wider goals I seek. But dedicating my everyday choices in service of world peace or greater joy does not seem to make a difference through thought alone. Thinking by itself is not enough. Spirit-filled choices are embodied choices, rooted through their blend of heart and mind and action. They take shape through a myriad of everyday relationships and choices. When I add in a measure of delight and joy, my choices come alive in a way that is spirited, uniquely personal and universally life-affirming.

But large goals such as peace and freedom from fear don't rely on us alone. They are served by a collective weaving, a confluence of individual acts interconnecting to inform and shape a healthy world. Like streams merging into a river, our choices and actions add strength and power to the flow. New collective possibilities emerge from the energy of our individual lives.

How to best meet these larger-than-my-life commitments? A phrase from the movie, Mary Poppins by Disney has been of great support for me in this. "Enough is as good as a feast." This bit of wisdom always brings me back to the next step in front of me. It is teaching me to look at what is enough and available to act on in the immediate moment. Planting my commitment in my heart, I take the next step.

This book suggests practices to put into action in your daily life. They are offered as starting points for your own discovery with the hope they will speak to next steps you can take to nourish your relationship with the spirited life within and around you.

Freya Secrest
June 2017

WRITER'S NOTE

Many of these practices are adaptations of my own and my colleagues' work with Incarnational Spirituality, a worldview that recognizes the earth and everything within it as sacred. Incarnational Spirituality posits that each of our lives is a valuable gift, to be honored for its unique expression. This is basic to its perspective. Secondly, it recognizes uniqueness is important. Our differences are valuable; they require respect. Third, Incarnational Spirituality affirms we exist in a universe that is dynamic, requiring an attitude of interest and openness. Fourth, it asserts that it is important to make space for collaboration; spirituality is a partnering activity.

The phrases and practices are divided into two areas—Particularity and Possibility. Like yin and yang, these two complements shape our wholeness.

You may notice some words used in unconventional ways. This is an intentional expansion of their meaning so that they reflect more dynamic interaction.

The term *felt sense* refers to your full body impressions. These can show up as sensations, images or memories. We invite you to be playful and explore the information your senses offer. This material is experiential, it is meant to be engaged.

When referring to the deeper experience of our individuality I have capitalized the "S" in the words "mySelf" and "ourSelves". There is a fundamental, sacred quality of Self that this book seeks to recognize and honor.

Freya Secrest

DESIGNER'S NOTE

The phrase *Let's stay in touch!* captivates me.

Touch can be other, external, or an activity outside of ourselves. It is often seen as an outside pressure, as something happening to us instead a state we are *in*, immersed *in*, embody*ing*. What is it to be *in* touch?

I explore this question through being present, using my senses, listening to my body and making space. I've found that being *in* touch is vital—whatever is happening it is touching me **now**. No matter how challenging, it is my present. It is my gift.

The vitality of my explorations is captured by presenting these discovery practices within luxuriously spacious layouts. I created the artwork and icon graphics to further enhance this effect.

My aim is to visually support you in staying present to these practices. I've designed open space where you may touch *in* with your gifts waiting to be opened, your **now** moment when you reach out your hand and introduce yourself.

Hello present, let's keep in touch.

Lyra Ziegler

HOW TO USE THIS BOOK

write it out

journal

take notes

connect ● the

dots

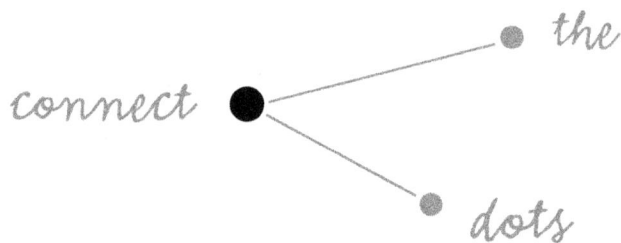

fill up
the margins

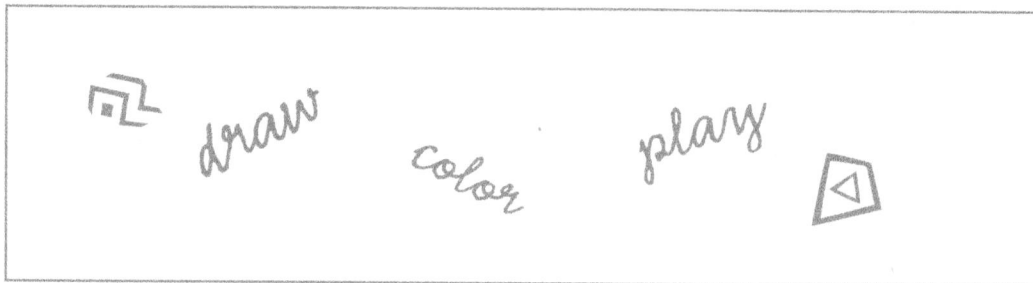

draw   color   play

This book includes 26 phrases intended to focus your attention on a particular practice or skill in being present to the sacredness within all life, including yourSelf. These practices have grown out of my experience. I encourage you to try them out and adapt them to your own situations. Let them develop in ways that nourish and expand you.

The activities included invite you to engage your discovery process through mind, body and heart. You might be asked to write a poem, move in space or draw an image. Color the shapes, record notes in the margins, make the book your own.

The Resource section includes some references for your further exploration. The book's practices reflect my exposure to a wide variety of materials from psychology, the arts, the spiritual and mystical, and the sciences. The references here are certainly not a comprehensive list but they suggest the broader context of ideas I have drawn upon.

COMMIT TO ALIVENESS

Anyone can manifest sacredness. It's not an evolutionary state per se—that is, I don't have to be evolved spiritually (whatever that may mean) to manifest the God Dimension, to be a deliberate "God-Keeper". I mainly need to deliberately manifest in my life as much of the presence of that dimension or the qualities of that dimension as I can—and usually we do that by being loving, compassionate, kind, joyous, and so on.

We do it by being life-affirming.

David Spangler

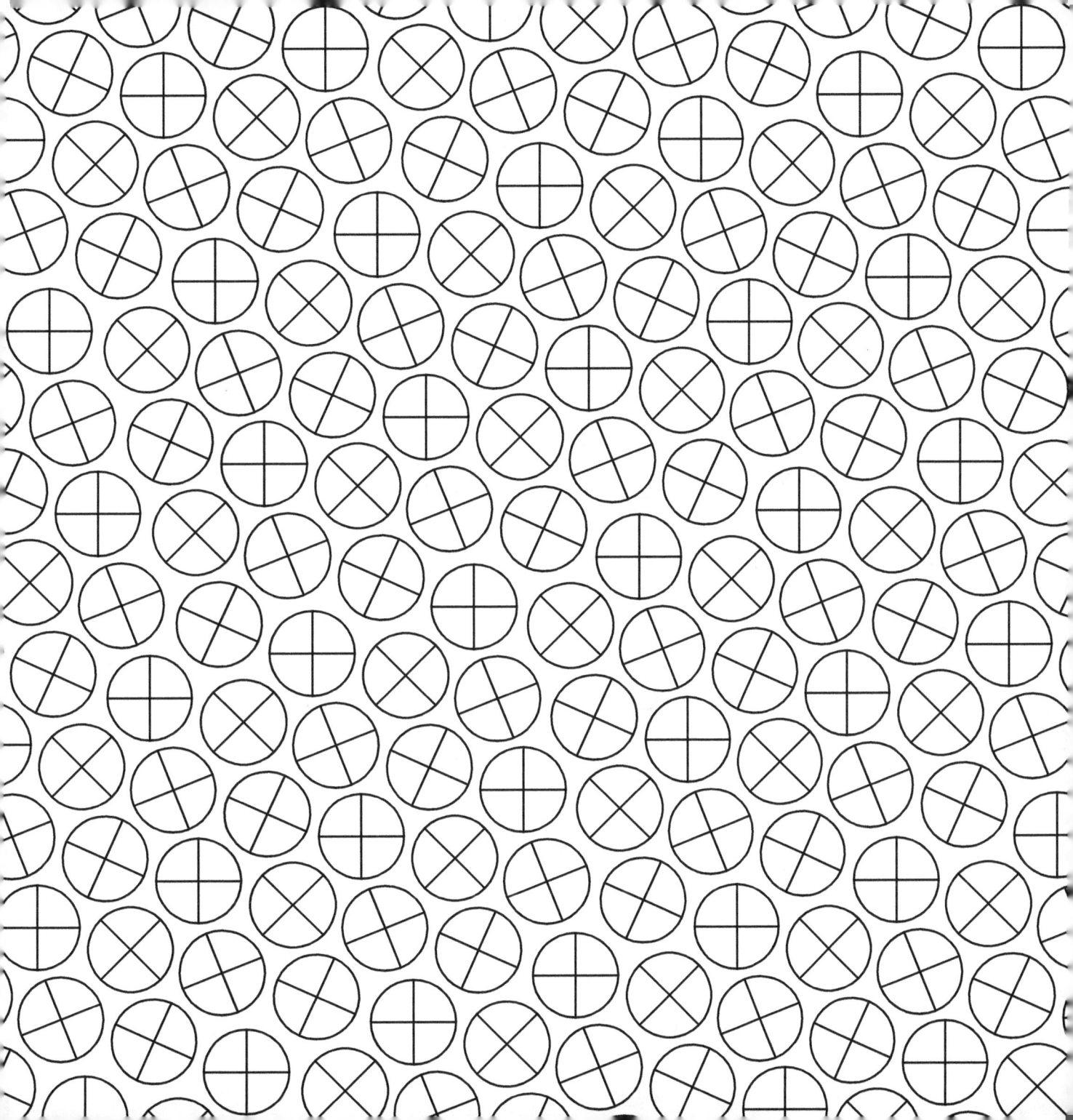

I believe in
the value and sacredness
of an individual life.

My personal choices and
experiences unfold into a
unique expression of life.

PARTICULARITY

I have the resources within me to live my life in fullness. Standing simply and completely in my strengths and weaknesses, I am enough; I have the capacity to fulfill my life's promise.

The heroes and heroines in stories have something to learn about themselves, about finding and using their particular gifts, and so do I. I am called to embrace the unique circumstances, patterns and relationships that comprise my life.

I AM SOVEREIGN: INDIVIDUAL BUT NOT ISOLATED.

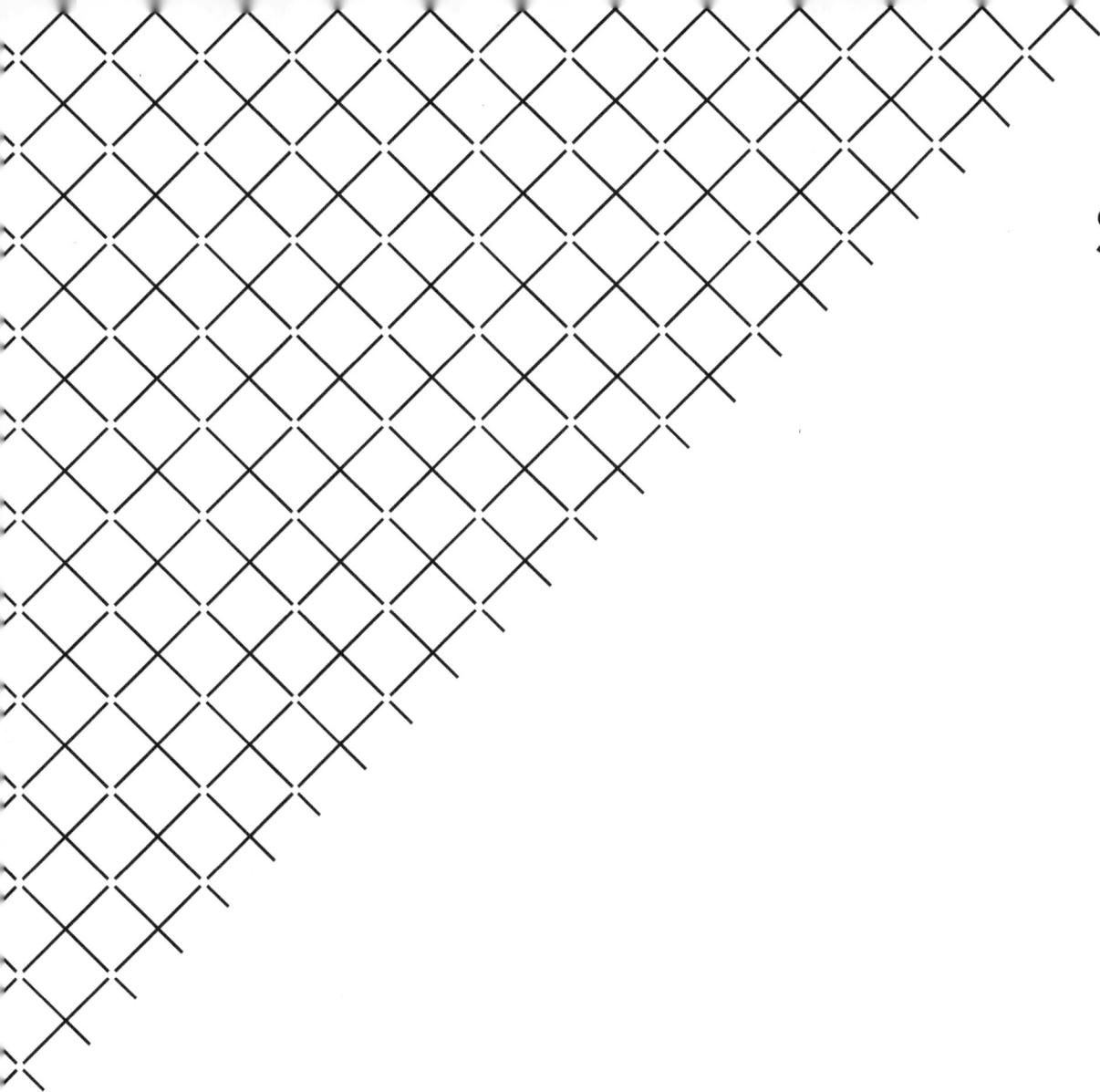

SELF

An individual consciousness;
the art of celebrating uniqueness.

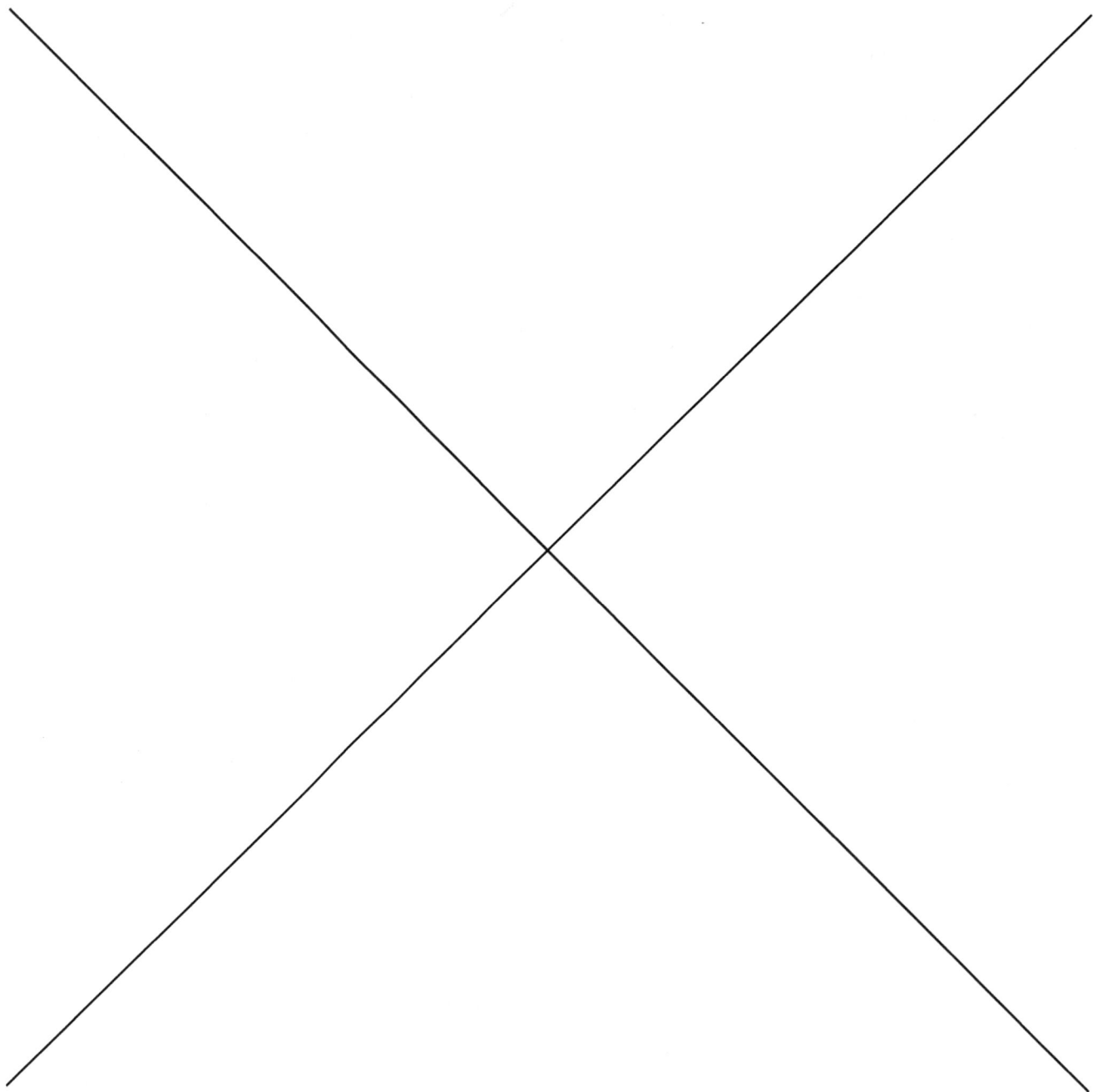

Stand up. Step out and take up as much space as possible, arms and legs spread wide. Then come back to standing at ease.

WHAT DO YOU NOTICE?

HOW DOES IT FEEL TO STAND UPRIGHT AND AT EASE?

TO STEP OUT AND TAKE UP SPACE?

SOVEREIGNTY

(SOV'ER EN TE)

The individual capacity to be fully oneself in the world while in relationship to the greater whole.

How do you know yourSelf?

When we think of our "Self" it is natural that we think of "who we are"—that is, our memories, our dreams, our joys and challenges, our skills, accomplishments and trials. We know ourselves through our experiences in the world. This is a good place to begin.

Consider the experiences of your life. Take a moment to reflect on those that have had a significant impact. Things like a special friendship, or the place you grew up, the birth of a child, or the loss of a loved one. On this page note or draw the special "touchstones" that have shaped you. As you do so, take a moment to honor and recognize how each of these experiences has shaped your life.

Self is also an organizing activity. It creates patterns of interaction, a "selfing" that takes different elements and draws them into a wholeness, allowing them to exist and work together. We each have many different facets, for example a person can be a mother, a graphic designer and a wilderness advocate. By enhancing the qualities common to each of these roles we weave them into a coherent wholeness of Self, each of our facets supporting and highlighting the other.

On this page note or draw some of the values that weave through the various roles that shape your life. Think of qualities such as kindness, honesty, or generosity that are important to you. As you do so take a moment to celebrate each of them.

Showing up is about building a relationship with the interior landscape of our life. It is about welcoming and appreciating the different parts that make up who we are and the varied and unique experiences we have. Drawing upon the truth of what we know we are able to stretch into the possibilities of who we want to be.

POSITION YOURSELF FOR PASSION

To know passion is to experience a deep, sometimes overwhelming flow of feeling and sensation. Passion brings color into the painting of our life; it energizes and enlivens.

I love walking outside when the wind is wild; I feel invigorated by the freshness and deeply connected with my body as I work to maintain balance in the push and pull of the wind's force. My passions are like that forceful wind that pushes me around if I'm not planted solidly on my feet. They can knock me off-balance if I am not working from a place of centeredness. The deeper I am rooted into the ground of mySelf the more capacity I have to creatively express my passion.

Consider a tree. We are usually most aware of the color and movement in its leaves and branches. But in order to support this canopy, a tree must have a strong trunk and a deep, wide system of roots. Similarly, our passions are the outermost expression of our core energy and resources. The more connection we have with our roots and trunk—those qualities and values we hold as central—the more life and vitality we have. When we stand grounded in what is deeply true for ourselves, our passions are fulfilled.

Discovery Practice: To stand on "our own two feet" is a gift of evolution. Take a minute to notice and appreciate your ability to stand upright.

If possible stand up. Be aware of your feet connecting you to the earth. Notice your arms free and flexible—able to reach out and interact. Turn your head side to side, eyes open, paying attention to how it feels.

Now take a moment to notice your spine, allowing it to align as naturally as possible. Let yourself physically and imaginally connect with the earth below your feet and the universe above your head. Feel the flow of energy that connects you. In standing you are an integral part of the universe, giving expression to its life energy. Come back to this practice at anytime to re-center yourself.

STANDING CELEBRATES UNIQUENESS

WHAT ARE THE IDEAS AND VALUES YOU STAND FOR, STAND ON?

WHAT ARE THE RELATIONSHIPS THAT YOU KNOW TO BE TRUE, THAT YOU CAN REALLY COUNT ON?

WHAT ARE YOU PASSIONATE ABOUT?

Reflection: Create a quiet space for yourself where you won't be disturbed. Take a few deep breaths. Consider your answers to the questions on the previous page.

What ideas and qualities came up for you? Which relationships came to mind? How do you experience these connections? How do your passions come alive in your life?

Your responses give a picture of your personal system of values, relationships and passions. This is a resource you can draw on.

Bring to mind a time when you acted on one of your values.

What do you notice in your body? Is there a particular place that responds to this memory? Does it carry a scent or color or flavor for you? Become familiar with this *felt sense* of your values as they live in you.

Now reflect upon your relationships and passions in the same way.

Doing this reflection on what really matters in your life is another way of standing, balanced in yourSelf.

JUICE UP YOUR JOY

Experiences that give me joy are a wellspring of energy in my life that is much more effective than coffee. And it is a source that I can tap into at will by choosing to focus on even the smallest encounter with delight. My energy increases and so does my sense of well-being, my patience and my ability to come up with creative solutions to problems. It is both useful and purposeful to give myself permission to show up to joy.

Discovery Practice: Settle into your quiet space. Take a few deep breaths and call to mind a joyful experience you have had. Remember the situation as completely as possible, bringing the memory fully into the present.

What do you notice in your body? How does it touch your emotions?

Now call to mind, heart and body another similar experience, remembering it as fully as possible. Give yourself some time to remember your experiences of joy. Fill the letters with your notes.

TAKE SPECIAL NOTE OF WHERE AND HOW JOY TOUCHES YOU IN YOUR BODY.

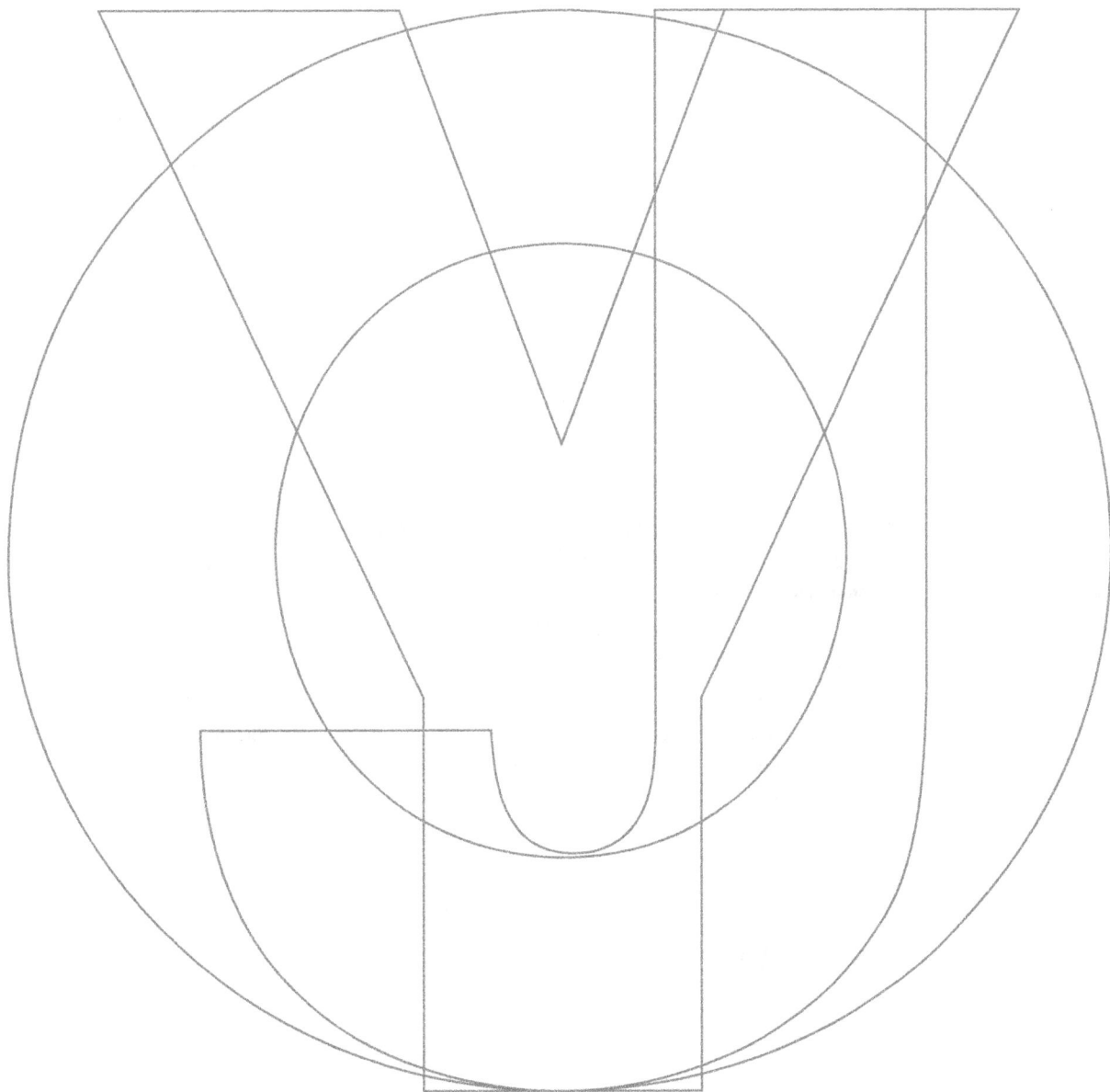

35 ✕

Discovery Practice: Juice up your Joy by coming back to re-visit your "joy" memories from time to time. Remind yourself of what is beautiful, delightful or richly rewarding in your world on a regular basis. These need not be big things; small moments will do. Notice the pleasure of washing your hands in warm water, the feel of clean sheets, the warmth from a fire, or perhaps the satisfaction of completing a task. Let the picture of a shared experience bring back the pleasure of time with loved ones. Keep your energy real and juicy by continuing to add to your personal pool of joy-connected moments and recalling them through memory, feeling and body awareness. Fill in what juices up your joy in the letters on the next page.

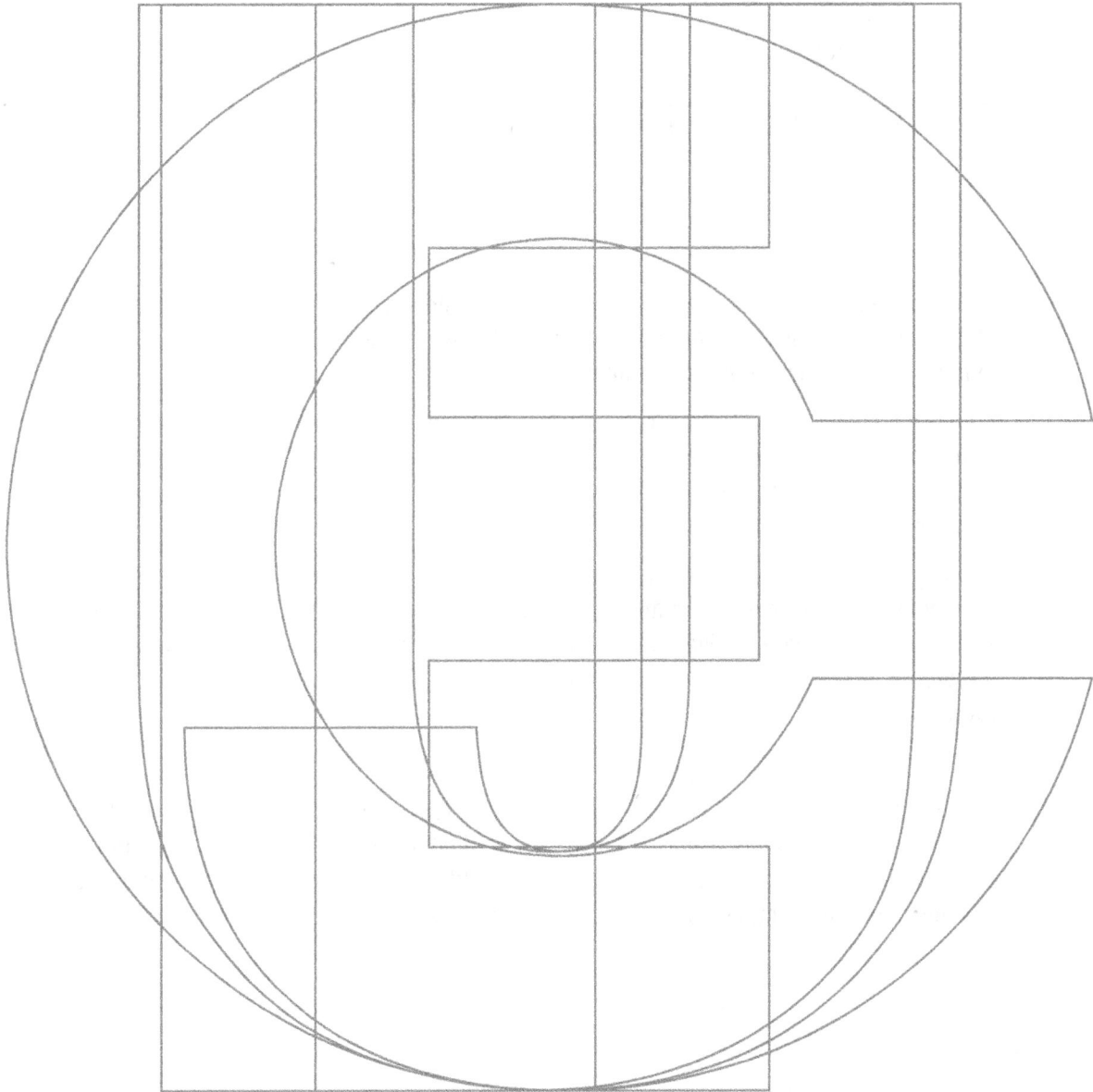

ACTIVATE PRESENCE

Many exercise programs now speak about activating and strengthening our core – that group of interconnected muscles in our torso that helps to maintain the integrity of our body's power to move. We activate and build that muscle group by repeatedly choosing to use it.

Presence is another aspect of our core structure. It is the interconnected configuration of commitment, intent, values, dreams and knowing that powers our life. We activate our presence by recognizing and engaging what is true for us, what frees us to give expression to ourselves in that situation.

One of my most useful practices to come back to a sense of wholeness is really simple—a 15 minute timeout. I might poke my nose outside for a breath of fresh air, or retreat for a short nap. It is not easy to give myself this time, but I have noticed I am more creative and resourceful when I choose to activate a connection to mySelf by creating a moment of open space.

Reflection: What practices have you developed to exercise presence in your life, to recognize what is true for you and act upon it? When you are tired, do you create a quiet moment for yourself or do you invite a friend for tea and a talk? When there is conflict or tension in your immediate environment, do you speak up or find another way to resolve the situation?

"Core spiritual strength as I see it is about developing and practicing the core wholeness of our incarnation. It is found in the presence of who we are as integrated beings, not just as physical beings on the one hand or spiritual beings on the other. If my core spiritual strength is diminished—and there are many ways this can happen in today's world—I am equally more vulnerable to the pressures and stresses, the impacts and diversions of life around me. I can lose my creative edge, my focus, my sovereignty, my capacity to serve. My boundaries become less healthy and useful and my ability to act with freedom in determining who I am and how I will connect to and bless my world can be subverted. Rather than being a co-creator with my world, I become an effect of my world. Happily, the presence of a core spiritual strength can be built up and developed just as our core physical strength can be. "

David Spangler

Discovery Practice: As you move through your daily activities please consider these questions:

WHAT CENTERS YOU?

WHAT SUPPORTS YOU?

WHAT FREES OR UPLIFTS YOU?

WHAT INVITES YOU?

These might be relationships, activities, places, attitudes or things special to you. These experiences of what is true for you strengthen your sense of presence and help you build energy, enthusiasm and meaning. Write your answers and add new ones as you identify them.

Now, in reviewing your responses on the previous page, I invite you to consider how you know these experiences center, support, free and draw you out. What are the indicators, the *felt sense*, you measure your experiences by? For example, what happens in your breath or in your posture? Is there a particular place or feeling in your body that indicates a state of ease or wellbeing? Do you notice this same response in several of your answers? Write a short poem about your place of ease using this suggested format:

Line 1—State the place of ease—*Knees relaxed*

Line 2—Describe what that makes possible—*Ready to move*

Line 3—Describe your state—*I am open to feel and respond*

Line 4—Repeat line 1—*Knees relaxed*

STACK YOUR GRATITUDE

Feeling grateful is an activity that allows me to pause, rest in appreciation and gather my resources before going on again. Stacking my gratitude brings to mind the mound of stones one might see piled on a beach when someone has taken the time to balance one on top of another. They are thoughtful sculptures bringing attention to connections. Showing up to what we are grateful for in our lives gives us time to celebrate our life and relationships.

Reflection: Create a space for yourself where you won't be disturbed. Sit quietly, taking a few slow breaths. Call to mind the things in your life for which you are grateful. They can be large or small; think of the song, "My Favorite Things" from the movie *Sound of Music*. Write your answers down on the next page. Try to write for at least 15 minutes. If you run out of ideas before the 15 minutes is up, sit quietly and wait to see what other memories might bubble up into your awareness.

WHAT ARE YOU GRATEFUL FOR?

Discovery Practice: Gather beads, shells, buttons or anything you wish and a string of your choosing. Seven to twelve beads create a nice size strand but you can use more if you would like. Draw from the list of the things you are grateful for as well as those that give you joy from pages 34-37. Identify one bead for each element you choose.

Draw or trace each bead or object you will use in the box below and name the element it represents.

CREATING YOUR PERSONAL GRATITUDE CHAIN

One of the great traditions of working with sacredness is the use of prayer or meditation beads. Contemplatives of many traditions use them regularly. This exercise invites you to make a string of gratitude beads using the experiences of joy and gratitude that empower you in your life.

Pick up a bead and hold it in your hand. Choose the first element or experience from your list and bring it fully to mind. Let the experience live in your body as you hold your bead, making an association between the two and then add it to your string. Pick up the next bead and as you hold it, attune to the element it represents. Add it to your string. Continue until you feel your gratitude string is complete.

Play with design, color and shape or keep it very simple. Each of the beads is like a seed for that element of joy or gratitude. Your gratitude beads are a unique reminder of the resources you have available. You might choose to make your bead string into a necklace or bracelet to wear.

AIR OUT YOUR ASSUMPTIONS

BREATHE.

Have you experienced a time when you thought you had a handle on a situation and then found you did not fully understand it? A time when you had jumped to an answer that did not fit the facts? Assumptions are blind spots in our thinking, places we no longer explore or refresh. They can be so intertwined in the structure of our thoughts that we do not recognize them as ideas which may no longer be true. Like a fish in water, I live in my assumptions without questioning them once they are established. And I have no real way of even noticing them until they are challenged by a situation that brings them into focus. My willingness to consider a question like, "What is possible right now?" opens up a window to begin to air out the assumptions I live with.

Airing out assumptions has a felt sense for me of hanging the laundry outside on a warm, breezy, sunny day. It feels fresh, direct, and honest. My breath deepens and intention gentles, creating spaciousness, interest and open possibility.

Discovery Practice: Create a sense of expansion and spaciousness with your breath. Exhale all the air out of your lungs, allow your body to take a deep breath. Now move into a rhythm of easy, deep breathing. For two minutes just pay attention to your breathing.

What do you notice?

How does your body respond?

Is there a place of tension you no longer need to hold?

Does your energy increase?

Note your responses to breathing on this page.

Engaging our world with a spirit of curiosity also helps us be present, cut through our assumptions and create space. When we meet the world with interest we do not take it for granted. Think of pushing back the curtains in the morning, meeting a new co-worker or even just opening up a fresh document on your computer. What do you notice in your attitude in these times of new beginnings? What questions come up for you?

Asking questions shifts my balance; my weight moves forward and up to the balls of my feet. I prepare myself to meet and respond to new information.

Discovery Practice: Set aside some time today to begin to explore a new interest you have. Perhaps it is something you have assumed is not possible for you to do (like writing a blog) or for which you have no known skills (like juggling) or something you are curious to know more about (like dolphins).

Think of three new areas of interest to you:

Pick one that you might work with in this next week. Write your interest in the circle on the next page. If you are interested in writing, what immediate activity would help move you toward that? If you want to find out about dolphins, where can you start—with a book, a TV program, a visit to the aquarium?

Finding the right question to open space and air out assumptions requires an attitude of interest. Which questions take you to the heart of your interest? Try queries that start with "How" or "When" or "What" before "Why". Write your questions around your topic and spend time this week exploring them.

LEAN INTO HUMILITY

Humility: from latin. humus – earth, ground, soil

To lean into humility is to be drawn into the greater continent of our lives, to recognize and honor ourSelves as one part of a whole.

No man is an island, entire of itself,
Every man is a piece of the continent, a part of the main.

John Donne

This quote by John Donne was part of a lesson in my sixth grade English class. These first two lines have stuck with me over time and come to mind whenever I need to remember that I am one element in the equation of the whole world. I am unique but not separate, distinct but not entire. How I recognize and act as one part of a wholeness is as valuable a part of self-knowledge as how I affirm my unique contributions to it.

Reflection: Take a minute to think about your discoveries about yourSelf in this section—what you know is true for you, your passions, your joys, the things you are grateful for, the things you are interested in and open up something new for you. Choose one of these elements and "lean" into it. Feel the gravity, the pull that connects you with this element of your life. Let yourself move with the pull. Center and choose another element. Try another, noticing what helps you to maintain a sense of balance as you lean.

Discovery Practice: Reflect on several of this sections discoveries from pages 24 to 45 and write them down next to one of the darker, inner dots in the center of these pages. Be present to these elements of your life; appreciate and celebrate these core parts of yourself.

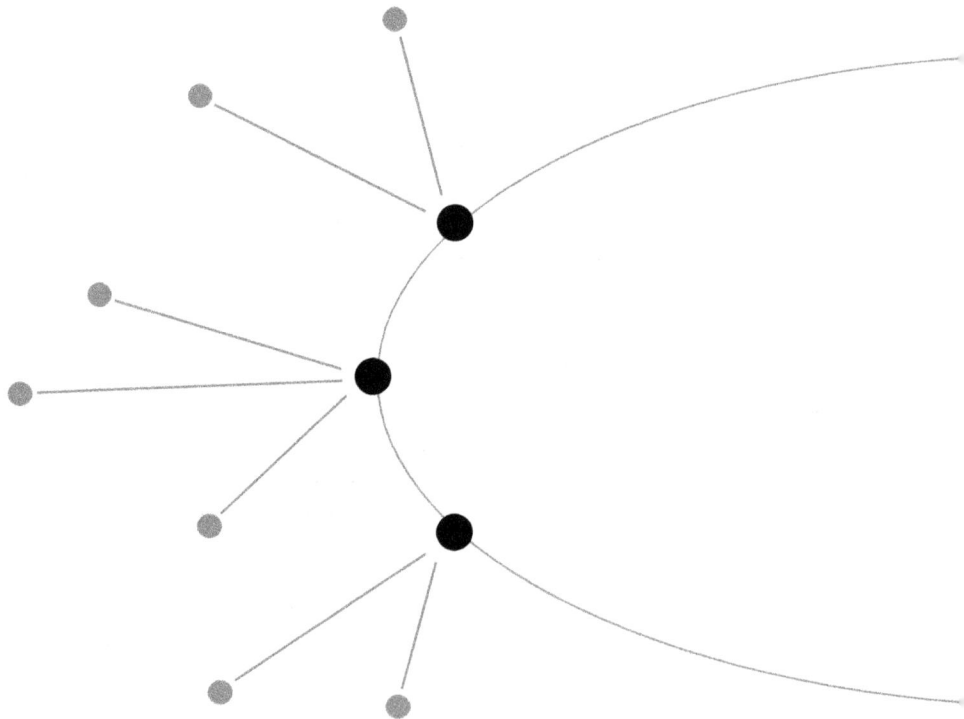

Now consider what person, place or experience in your life is connected to that part of
yourself. Is there someone or some experience that helped you to learn and integrate that
quality or lesson? How is it supported by the "continent" of your life? Write down that
connection from the wider field of your experience next to its linked dot. Take a moment to
appreciate and honor these partners in your life and learning. They are a part of you too.

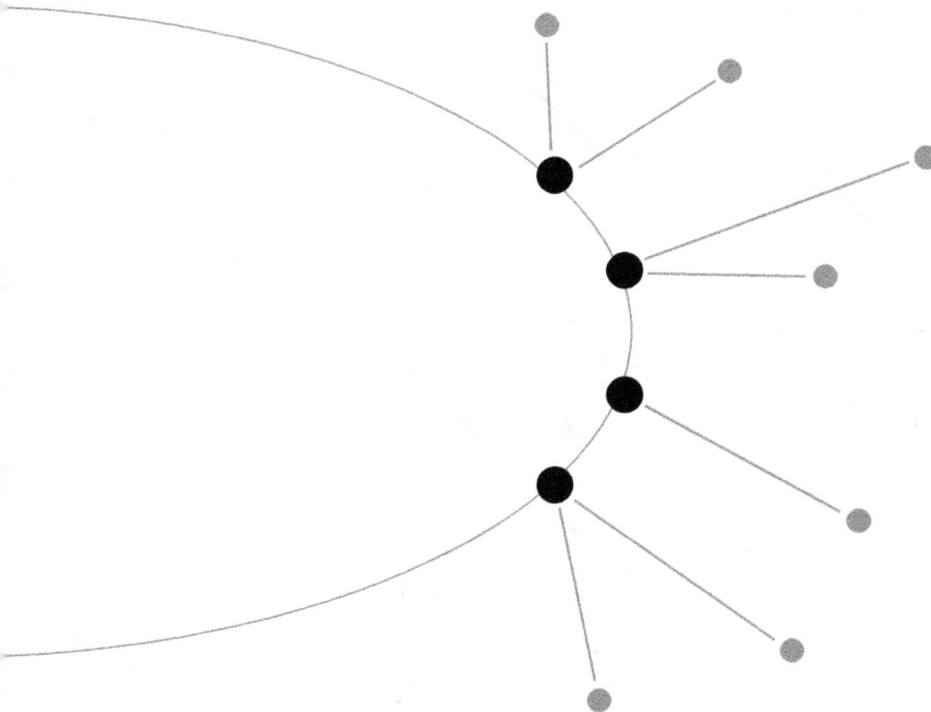

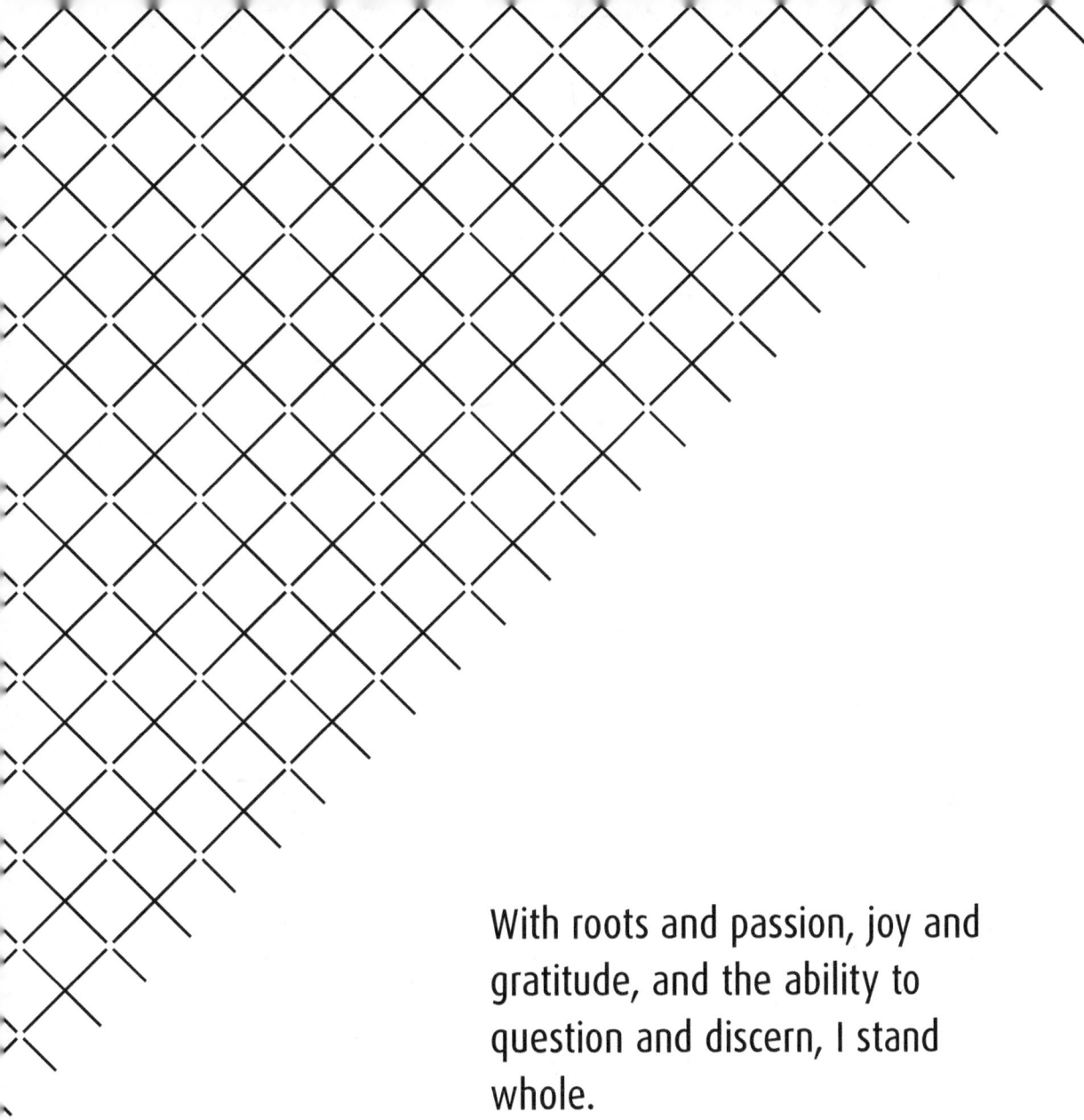

With roots and passion, joy and gratitude, and the ability to question and discern, I stand whole.

I am mySelf.

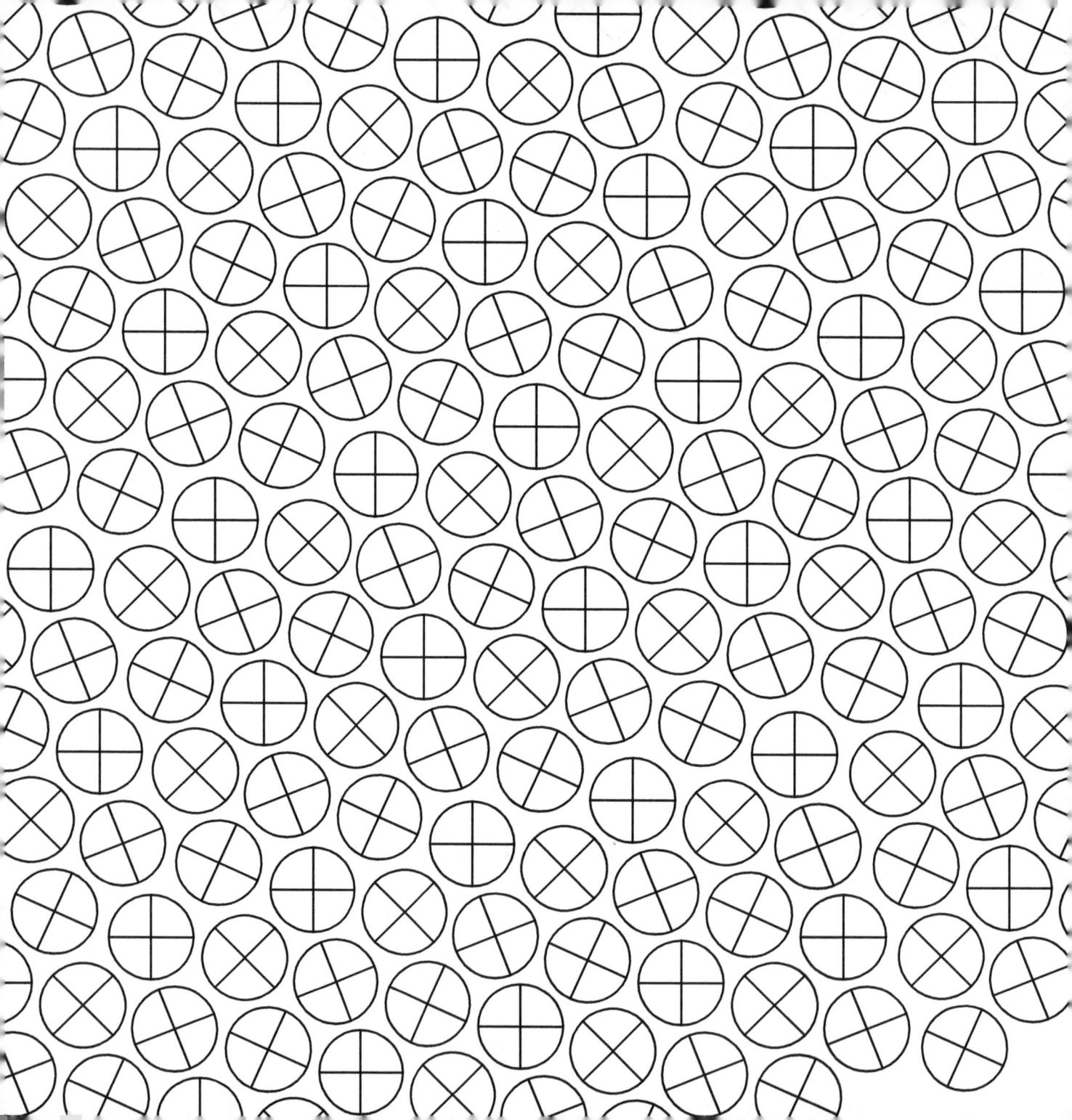

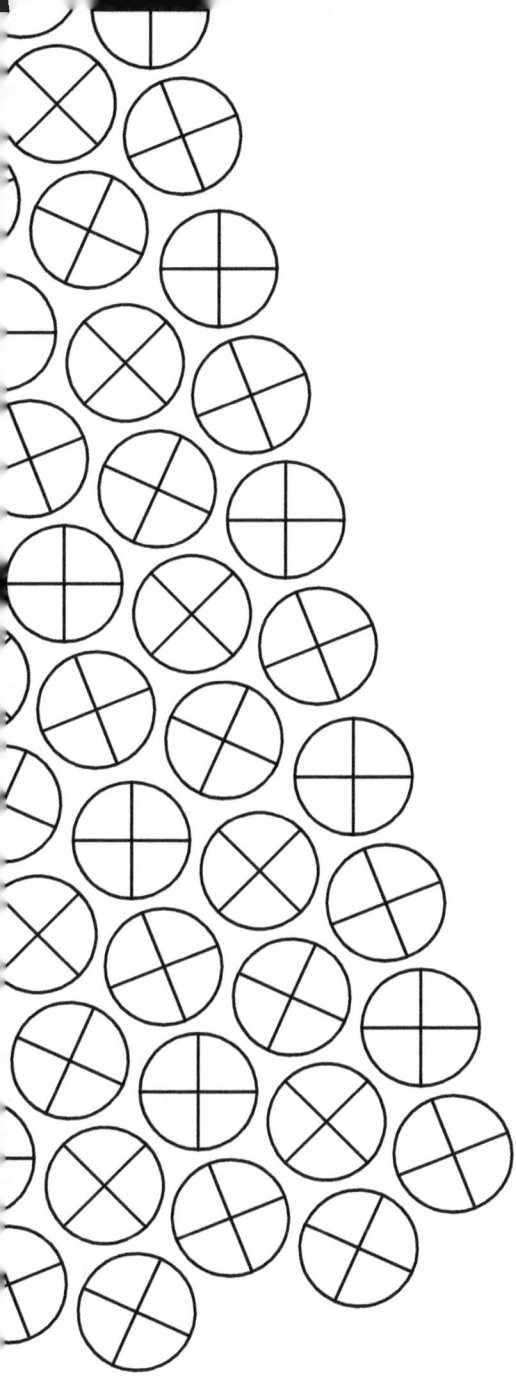

EDGE

A place where two things meet,
the art of honoring difference.

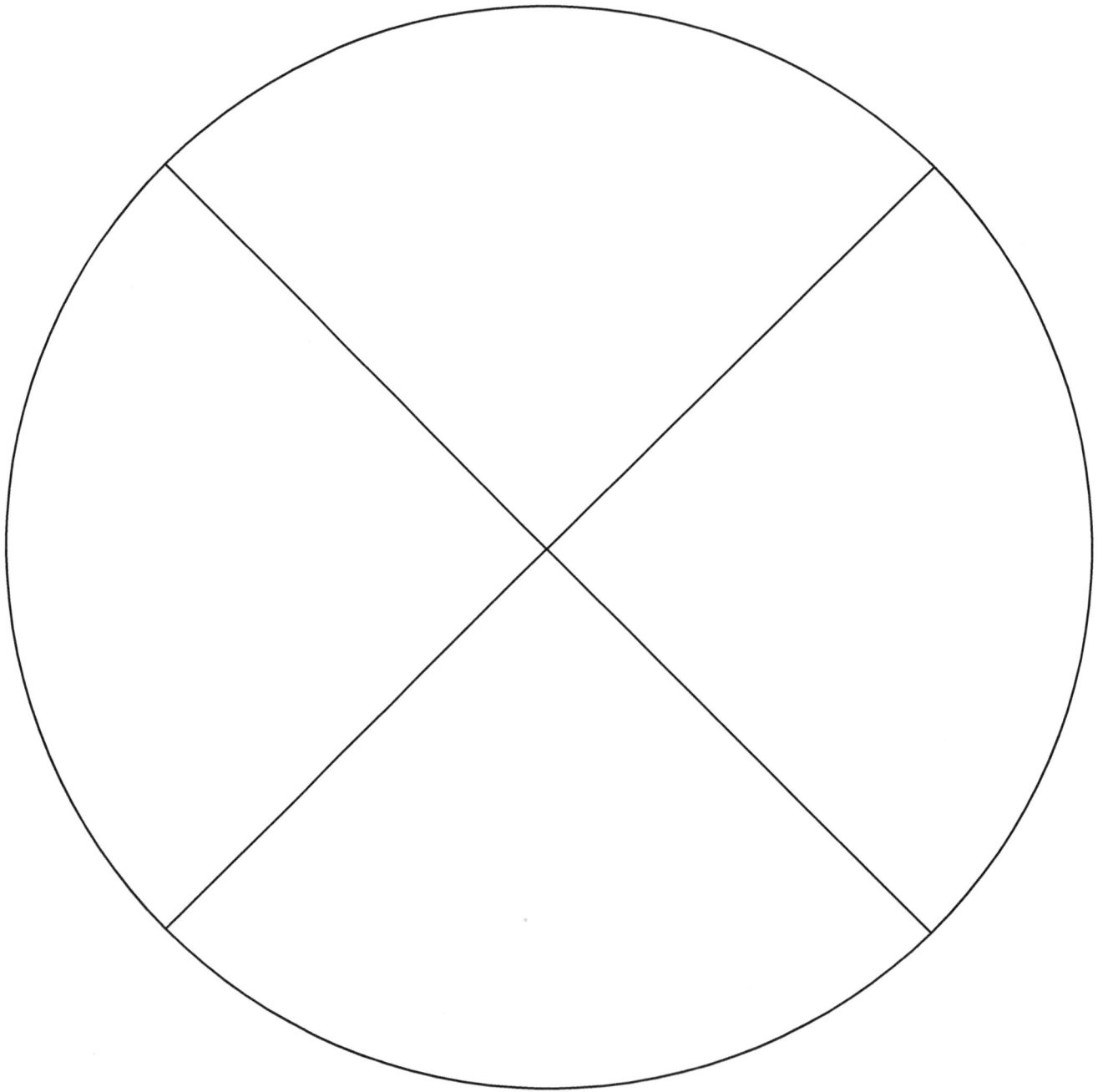

Sit in a chair with arms resting lightly on your knees. Notice the space that is created when you do so. Make the shape of an "o" by touching your fingertips together, elbows wide apart.

WHAT DO YOU NOTICE?

HOW DOES IT FEEL TO DEFINE SPACE IN THIS WAY?

WHAT IS THE DIFFERENCE BETWEEN THE SPACE INSIDE AND THE SPACE OUTSIDE YOUR ARMS?

RESPECT

(RI SPEKT')

Due regard for the feelings, wishes
and rights of self and other.

How do you honor yourSelf?

There are many different kinds of edges that define our lives: physical, mental, emotional, social, environmental—you may think of others. It is useful to be aware of our edges as boundaries that define and differentiate us. They help us to know what is part of us and what is not. Our edges create a container that shapes our focus and defines our activity. They create a safe place for us to show up as ourSelves.

Discovery Practice: Choose two of the values from your "How do you know yourSelf" exploration on page 29. Write one above each of the circles on the next page. As you write them down, think of a time you experienced that value and notice what conditions helped you embody it. What state of mind helped you to come to that place? How did the environment support you? Inside each circle write these nourishing conditions. Outside each circle write down what conditions take you away from your enjoyment of that value.

One of my values is joy. Working with color helps me to experience joy, but I have learned I must be clear about how much time or energy I have to focus on my color projects. I consider my boundaries of time and energy important because when I go beyond my available energy all enjoyment is lost. For example, in thinking of my joy in sewing, inside the circle I put "colorful quilts" because they engage me with color. Outside I wrote, "too big a project" thinking about how my available time influences my enjoyment.

_____   _____

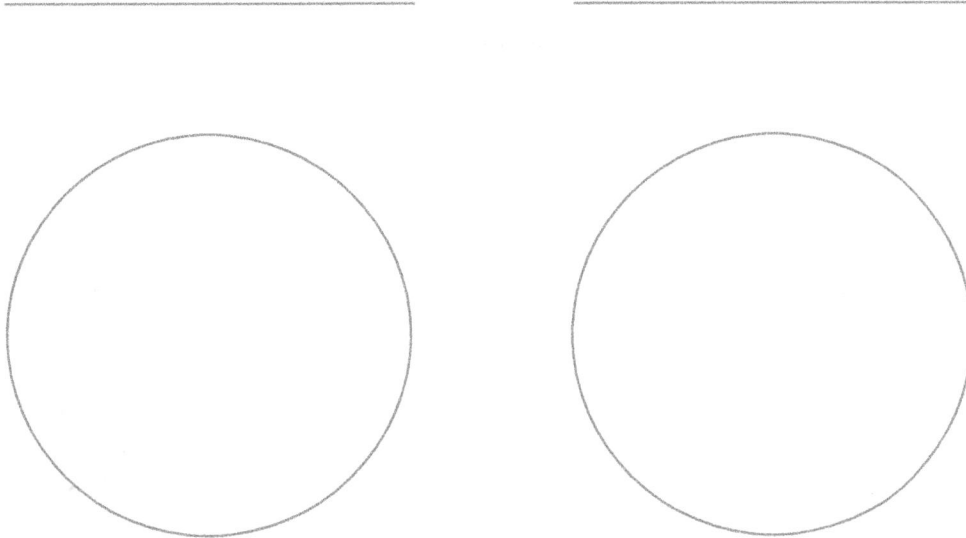

Edge is also a place of meeting. It is at our edge that we connect to other. The boundary line can be soft or hard depending on many things – timing, our energy level, our sense of affinity.

Where do you draw the line between what nourishes and takes away from your values? As you consider the boundary around each value what shape does it take? Is it a soft blending or a hard wall? Does the boundary around one value feel different than another?

Shade the edges of your circles to make them your own.

Showing up is not only being present to the interiority of our life, it is about our ability to meet our edges. It is at our boundaries that we connect to the world around us.

SAY NO TO NUMBNESS

As a can-do sort of person, I create long lists of tasks for myself to accomplish. Then to get everything done, I go into a state of overdrive that can leave me numb and exhausted. Once I worked myself to near collapse. After seeing me at that point a friend wisely told me that I could do anything but not everything. Learning how to follow that sage advice has been a journey that has introduced rhythm as a resource in my life. I can accomplish more if I balance activity with rest. When I attend to my need for a respite in the course of a day's tasks, I step away from the sense of pressure that numbs me and allows me to ignore the boundaries of my physical and emotional energy. Balancing rest and activity, I can be responsive, creative and present.

Reflection: Pay attention to the rhythm of your breathing. In between the inhalation and exhalation there is a short moment of rest for your lungs—a threshold moment between inbreath and outbreath. Consider for a moment the rhythm of your day and your times of rest, activity and the space between.

How do you take time to breathe in your day? Is there a moment, however long or short, that helps you "catch your breath" between different activities?

Discovery Practice: How do you know when you need to slow down and take a break? What is the internal sense that says to you, "You need a shift", either mentally, physically or emotionally? Is there a particular place or feeling in your body that indicates this state? For example, what happens to your breath? In your posture? What is your mental or emotional state?

WRITE THOSE SIGNALS HERE

_____

_____

_____

_____

_____

_____

Discovery Practice: Think again of things that give you joy, referring back to your answers on pages 34-37. Consider some particularly favorite things that help you rejuvenate. Which ones help you create a sense of rhythm and add to your sense of vitality and ease? Create your list below.

I have learned that taking a few deep breaths helps me slow down and collect myself. Another thing I do is begin to hum a tune. Humming introduces an element of flow into my body. I am able to step back from pressure and look at life differently.

THINGS THAT REFRESH ME:

Imagine a situation in which you feel blocked. Notice the response it creates in your body. Take an activity from your Things That Refresh Me list and put it into action. Allow that which encourages rhythm to help your energy begin to move and flow.

After a few minutes, imagine your blocked situation again. How does it feel in your body now? Can you see possibilities that weren't there before? Do you have more energy to focus on the problem?

Look over your list again. What is the activity you use most often? Put a star by it.

What is your second choice? Circle it.

Lastly, what is your fallback activity, the easiest thing you can do when you are stuck? Underline it.

Having a list of your refresh options helps you remember how to maintain rhythm when life gets stressful and takes you out of normal routines.

COMPLIMENT THE AWKWARD

"Positivity is a condition of being radiant, open, giving, confident, and strong. It is an energy state as much as a psychological one. It is enhanced by valuing and honoring yourself and standing in your uniqueness and sovereignty."

David Spangler

A compliment is an expression of praise or respect. I know that when I receive a compliment and really take it in, it warms me. My sense of what I am capable of doing or being expands; I bloom. The value of a compliment is not so much in its focus on a specific detail but on the overall feeling of being held in a positive light.

What about those parts of ourselves that are still learning and growing, still trying to figure out how to act in a situation?

When we are able to show respect for our awkward parts and embrace them with positive regard, we begin to expand and grow.

Discovery Practice: Close your eyes and imagine yourself held in a space of warmth and hospitality, a place where you feel at ease. It could be outside in a natural setting; it could be sitting in a favorite chair. Take a minute to settle into that space. Let the atmosphere of appreciation and warmth touch and fill all parts of yourself. How does your body respond? Mark the *felt sense* of this space so you can step into it again.

Now, imagine a friend and envelop them in the same spacious aura of warmth and possibility. See this person in a space where they can relax, stretch and expand in the wisdom and guidance of their own inner intelligence and spirit. Spend a few minutes holding this space for your friend.

Now imagine someone you don't like. Centered in your own sense of balance, joy and ease offer them hospitality. There is no need to try to heal them or change them. Imagine them in an open space that offers room to expand, where they are guided by their own inner intelligence and spirit.

Reflect back on your experience of being held in a space of ease. Choose a color that carries the feeling of what you experienced. Imagine that color filling the space around you. What compliment can you give to yourself?

Think of your friend. Choose a color that carries a feeling of warmth and possibility. Imagine that color filling the space around them. What compliment can you offer them?

Now think of the person you don't like. Again, choose a color that carries a feeling of hospitality. Imagine that color filling the space around them. Is there a compliment you can give them?

When you are finished take a breath. Center yourself with the standing practice on page 31 before moving on.

AMAZE YOUR BED BY MAKING IT

How often do you make your bed, really make your bed, tightening corners and smoothing covers? We use down comforters in our household which makes it easy to hop out of bed, flick a corner to slightly straighten the puff, and head out quickly into the day. But on those days when we change the sheets and take time to make the bed with some intention, I find I take great pride in consciously straightening and arranging the covers. When I pass through my bedroom on an errand later in the day, I find I notice a difference. The room is calmer, more inviting and restful. I too am calmer, more integrated and balanced in myself.

My bed holds me for one third of my day. It supports my dream life, my love life and my physical renewal. My attention to straightening the bedding is a small but significant act of connectedness. In that moment, I link with an attitude of respect and partnership that stays with me and ripples out into my day. Attending to my bed becomes a meaningful spiritual practice.

Discovery Practice: Make your bed with intention—or choose another daily task you do and bring your respectful attention to that work. Ask yourself how your efforts highlight the function and service of that object or activity. Appreciate its contribution to your life. Does your attention make any difference in the environment or in your relationship to the work itself?

Write down or draw any reflections about your experience.

My friend Dorothy Maclean tells a wonderful story about learning to bring love into her daily tasks. Dorothy worked as a secretary and spent much of her life in an office which was challenging for her as she loved nature and being outside. She also studied with a spiritual teacher who taught that "work was love in action" and would not have her students around her when they were in an unloving state of mind.

One day typing at her office desk, Dorothy noticed she was feeling resentful. She did not want to be inside that office, the typewriter was being temperamental, and nothing was flowing smoothly. It was hard to feel loving in her situation.

But she wanted to change her attitude and live up to her "love-in-action" training so she considered—was there anything at all she could love in her situation? Looking around she noticed the color of the walls—a warm yellow that she herself had chosen. Looking at those yellow walls, she felt a loving response. That simple connection to a color she loved flowed out and helped her to shift her attitude toward the tasks she needed to do. Her work in the office began to flow more smoothly and soon after other opportunities began to open up that took her away from office work.

DISCOVERY PRACTICE: WHAT HAPPENS WHEN YOUR WORK BECOMES YOUR "LOVE-IN-ACTION"?

WHAT OPENS UP FOR YOU? WHAT OPENS UP IN YOU? SHARE SOME OF YOUR EXAMPLES HERE

_____

_____

_____

_____

_____

_____

_____

_____

_____

_____

CUDDLE UP TO FEAR

To cuddle is to get close enough to connect with someone or something. If we cuddle we can enfold and be warmed by shared space and attention.

Can you think of a time you enjoyed a cuddle? A time when you shared a space that brought warmth and connection? Maybe it was a time sitting with your cat purring on your lap, or your child snuggling with you as you tucked them into bed? As you re-imagine that experience, notice how that moment of connection lives in your body. Does it have a shape or color, quality or texture? Draw or describe your *felt sense* of cuddling on the next page.

EXPLORE YOUR FELT SENSE OF CUDDLE

Curiosity: from latin. cura — to care

Curiosity opens a door that might lead us to care about something. To care is to be interested and interest allows us to build a connection.

To cuddle up to something is to affirm our connection to it and create an open and inclusive space where we feel free to love. When we "cuddle up" to something that is unknown to us, to something that we might fear, it is helpful to engage our curiosity to get to know it better first.

Discovery Practice: Take a few breaths and settle into a place of centeredness and ease. Hold yourself in a loving space. Imagine your pet or a loved one cuddling with you. Let the warmth of that space fully surround and enfold you.

Now imagine a recent time when you felt slightly nervous or anxious. Invite that experience to come forward to the edge of your space, but only as close as feels comfortable. If this experience had a color, shape or size what would it be? How does it move?

Do you notice any new information that helps you better understand your discomfort? Hold your connection as long as you care to and then release the experience.

Take a breath. Center yourself with the standing practice on page 31 before moving on.

Bring this anxious experience to mind again and notice if or how your response is different. Note your discoveries below.

_____

_____

_____

_____

_____

POLISH YOUR PATIENCE

Am I a patient person? If I'm honest I must say no, not really, but I do practice patience. Patience is defined as calm understanding and endurance but I experience it inside myself as a form of spacious resilience. Polished, patience reflects no judgement or blame, it stays present to what is. Patience is most possible when I respect my own boundaries. It asks me to know my priorities while at the same time respecting another's needs.

Reflection: Think of your own natural relationship to time. Do you process things quickly, eager to get "to the point"? Do you move more slowly, taking longer stretches of time? Are you consistent, moving step by step or do you jump from activity to activity?

Now, think of someone you know that moves in a different rhythm than you do: a friend, a family member or a co-worker. How do any differences impact your relationship?

WHAT HELPS YOU KEEP YOUR PATIENCE "POLISHED"?

Patience is a slippery thing.

It can often get lost or
slip through our fingers.

Discovery Practice: It is important to recognize and honor your own rhythms and values in order to keep track of your patience. To be patient requires a connection to what's important to you as well as what is important to others. Patience asks us to take ownership of our edges.

THINK OF A TIME YOU LOST YOUR PATIENCE

What were your needs in that moment?

Did you express those needs clearly?

What were the other person's needs?

Would you respond differently in the future?

EMBRACE YOUR ARTISTRY

I was not taught how to claim my own accomplishments. It was bad form to "toot your own horn" or celebrate oneself too loudly. But claiming our particular gifts and skills is the basis for creating a life. It is the foundation for our relationship with the world. When I embrace what I know of myself, my passions that say "Yes" and my edges that say, "Slow down", I show up in my creative power.

Discovery Practice: Fill in these statements in the circle about yourself. Draw and decorate the edge of your circle as a way to embrace them.

I AM _____

I ADMIRE _____

I LOVE _____

I CHERISH _____

I HONOR _____

I GENERATE _____

I OFFER _____

Discovery Practice: There are many ways to be an artist. What is it about the way you meet the world that you recognize as creative, innovative or impactful? For example, are you a good listener or an enthusiastic initiator?

How do you affirm the work you do and your particular way of doing it? Do you draw together lots of new ideas or are you someone who takes up a task and completes it? Artistry is not confined to those who dance or make music. It is about the quality of attention you bring to any task.

Celebrate your artistry by recording some of the particular ways you that you express it.

Write an appreciative thank you card to yourself drawing on the responses you wrote on pages 85 and 86. Mention the specific things you do in your life that reflect your particular gifts. Be appreciative of who you are in the world. Put your card in an envelope and mail it to yourself. When it arrives, sit down and read it.

Honor your life's artistry in the many ways it unfolds.

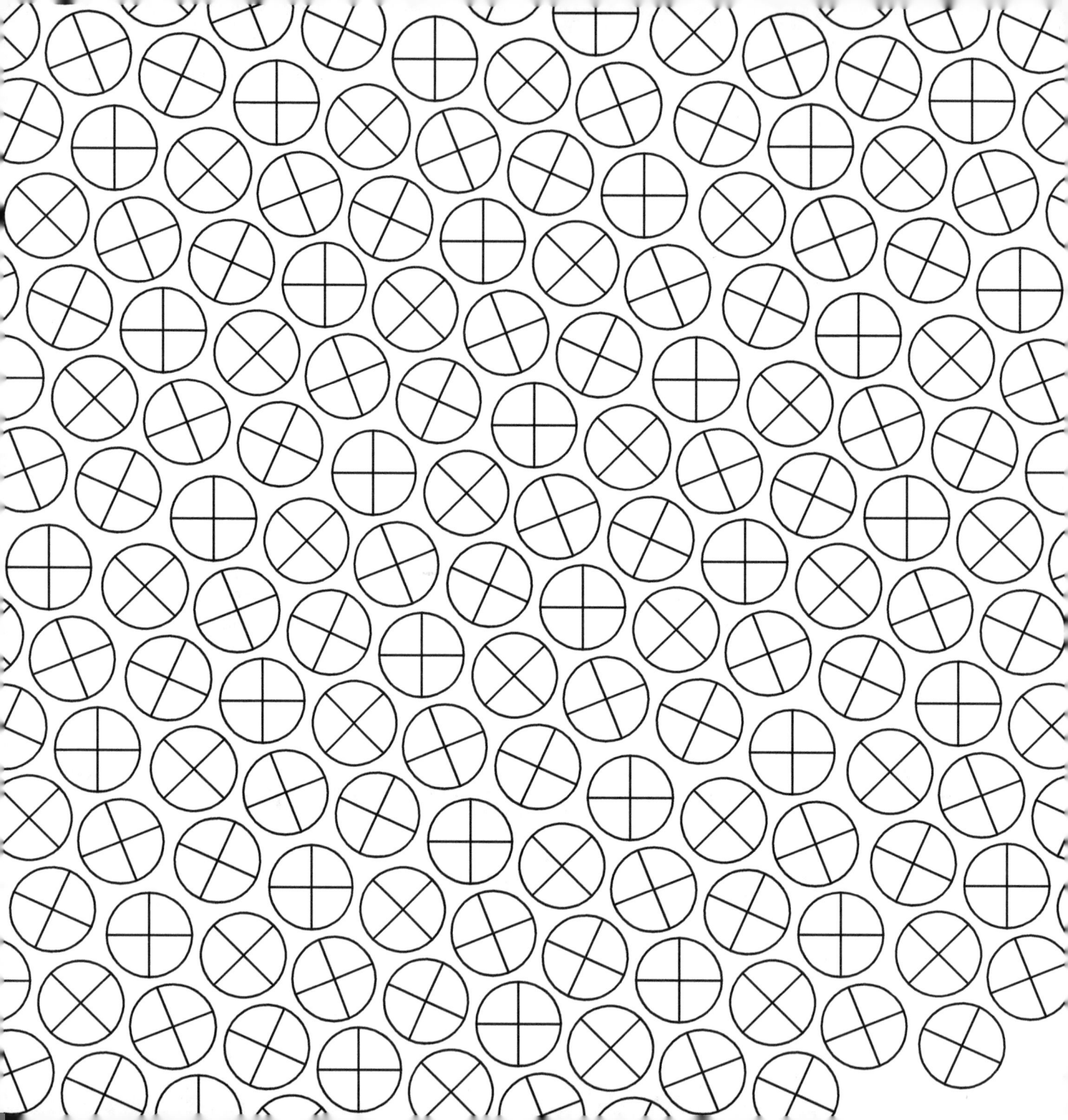

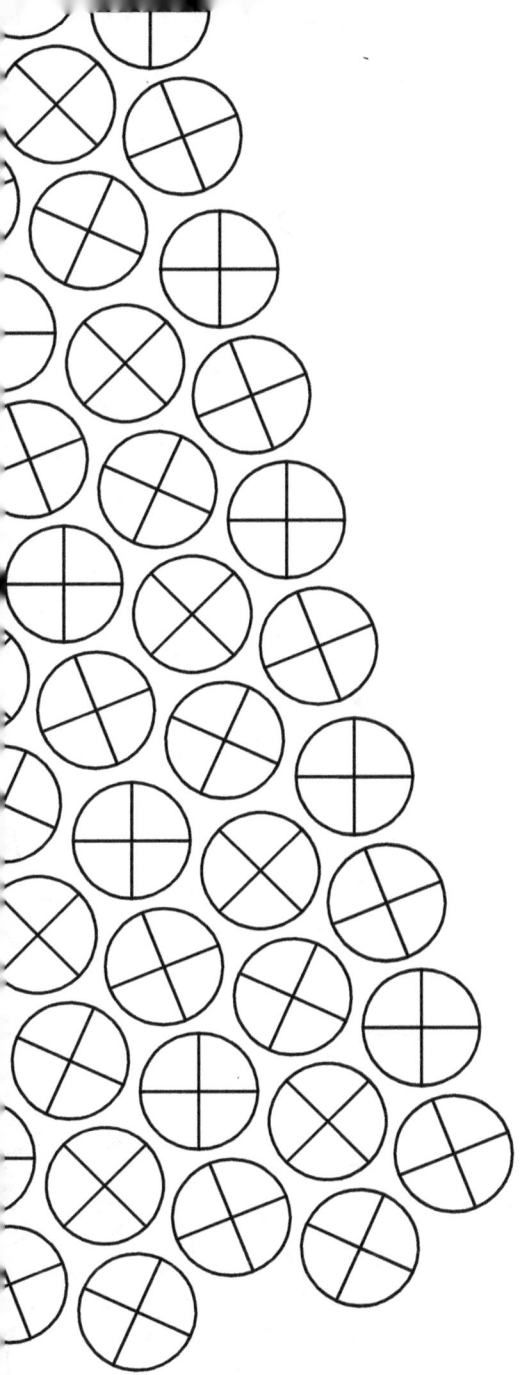

With rhythm and patience,
hospitality and care, and the
ability to respect my own
artistry, I define my life.

I celebrate mySelf.

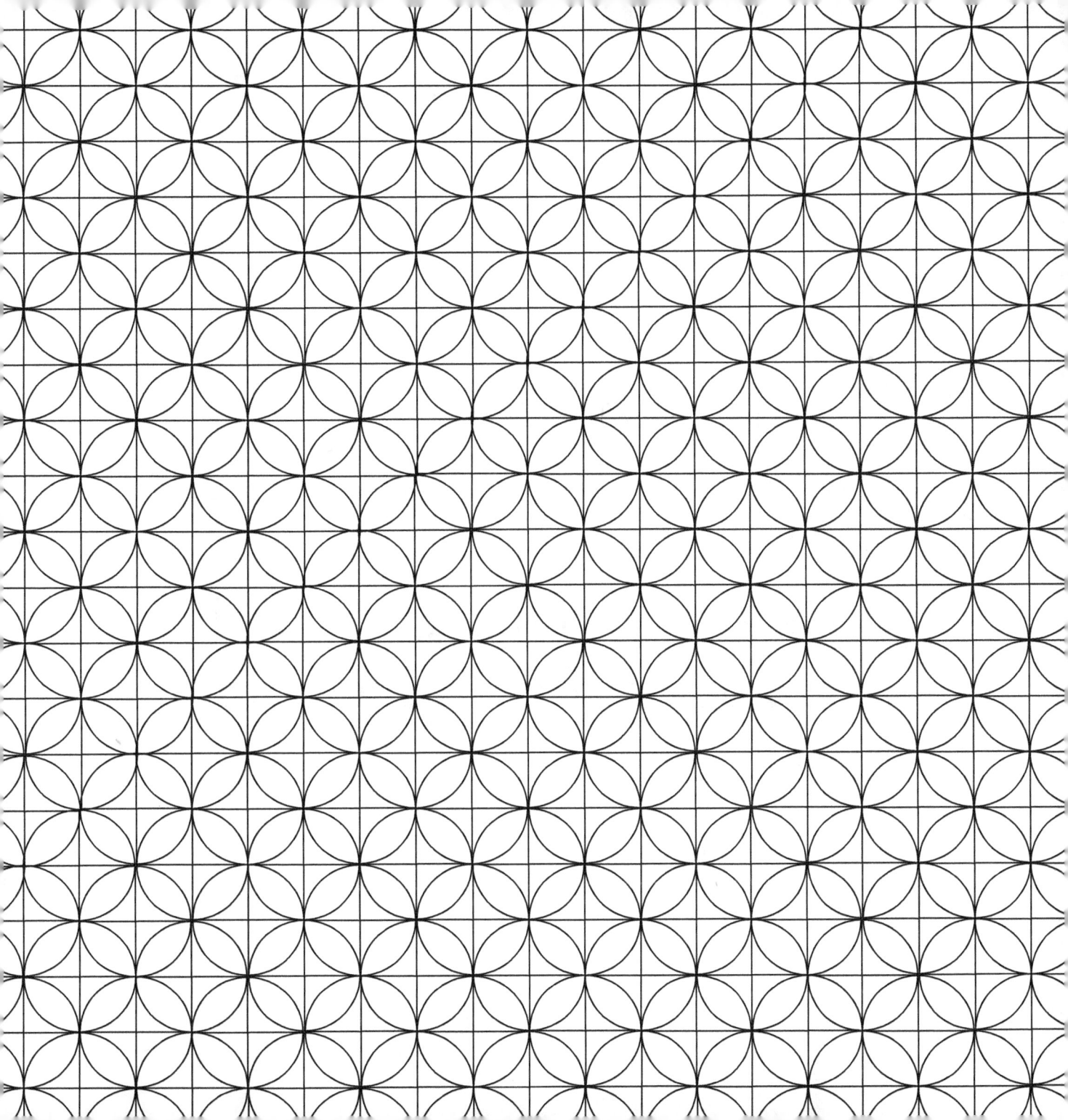

I trust in the creativity that unfolds from my connections.

My ability to respect myself and others opens the potential for newness.

POSSIBILITY

I have the opportunity to engage creatively through my life. Willing and resourceful in my curiosity, I welcome possibility. My world and I are discovering ourselves together.

My exploration calls me to trust, cooperate and engage. I am called to welcome the unknown from my own sphere of balance.

I AM SPACIOUS: OPEN YET FOCUSED.

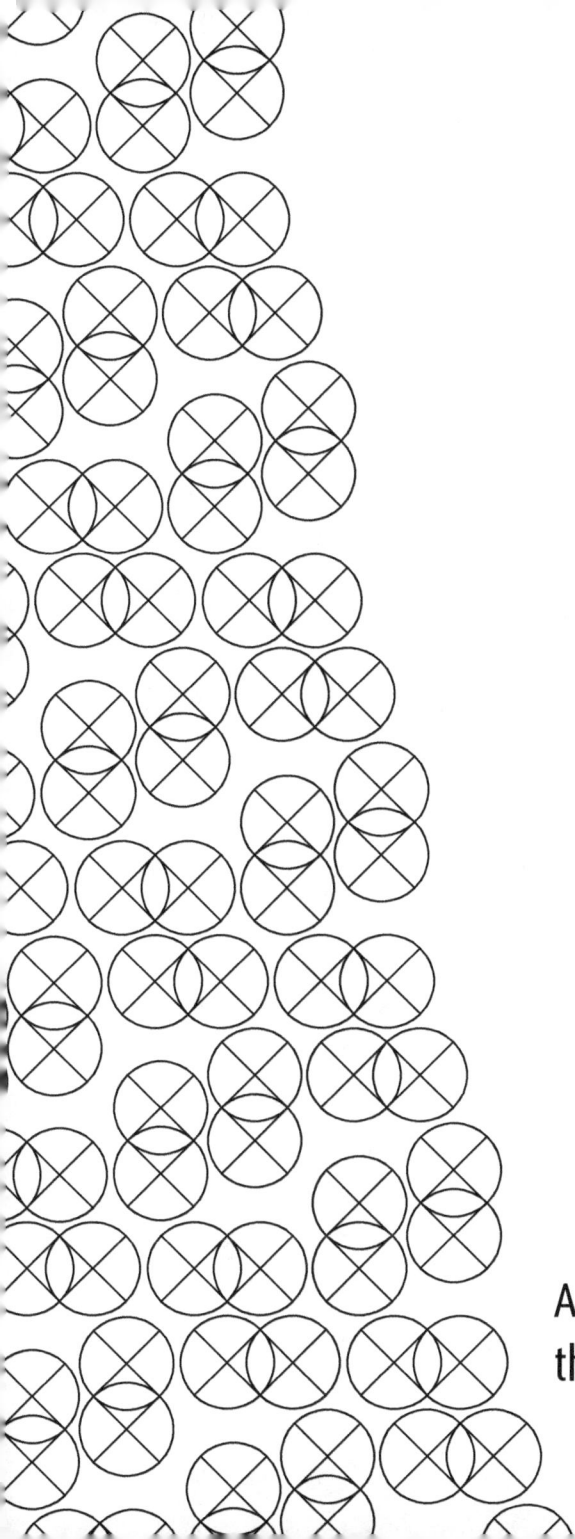

RELATIONSHIP

A process of interaction,
the art of connecting with another.

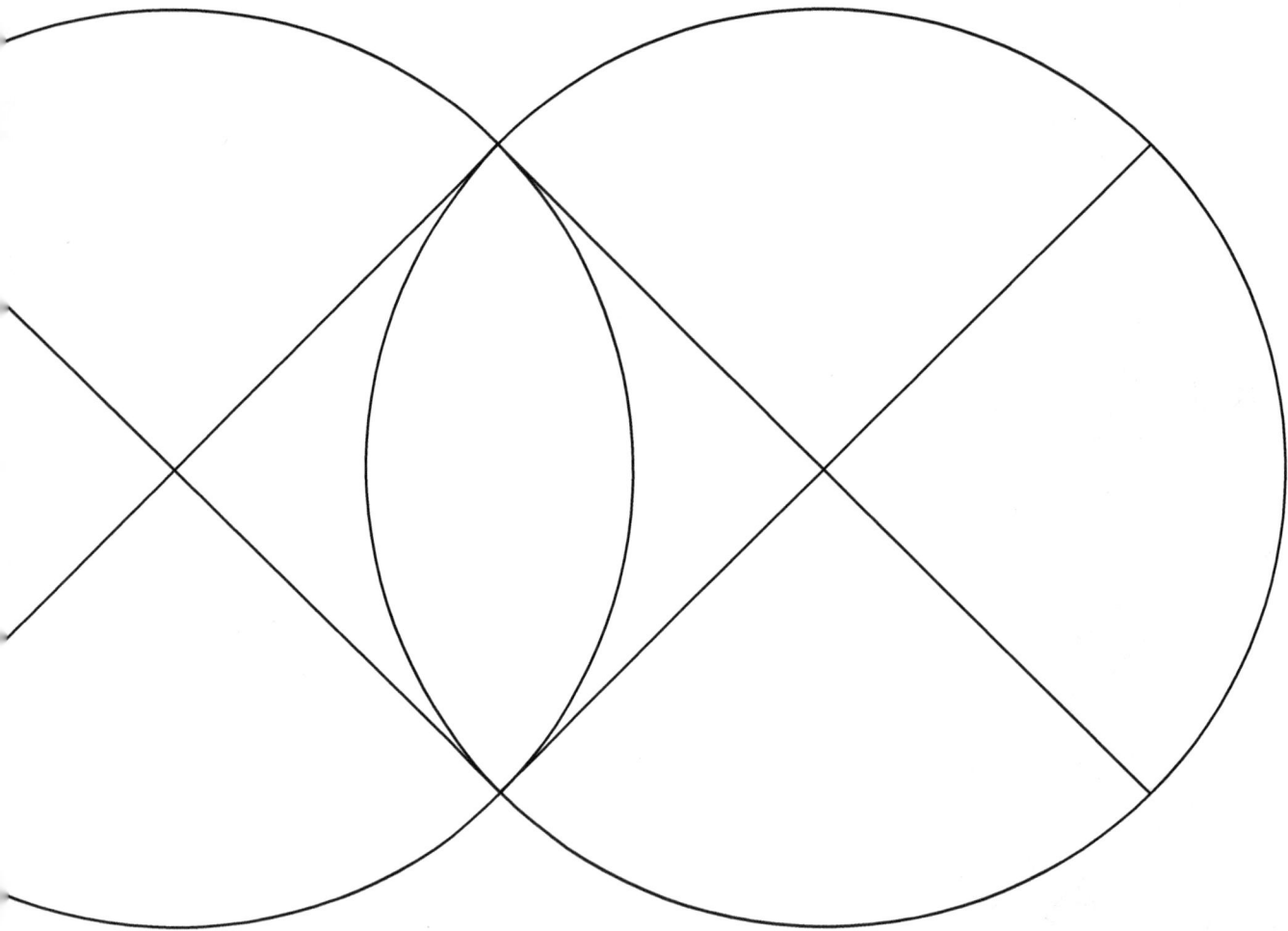

Imagine you are inviting a partner to dance. Step toward them and, looking directly "eye-to-eye", honor them by giving a bow. Imagine they are doing the same to you. Step back.

WHAT DO YOU NOTICE?

WHAT IS THE FELT SENSE OF HONORING YOUR PARTNER?

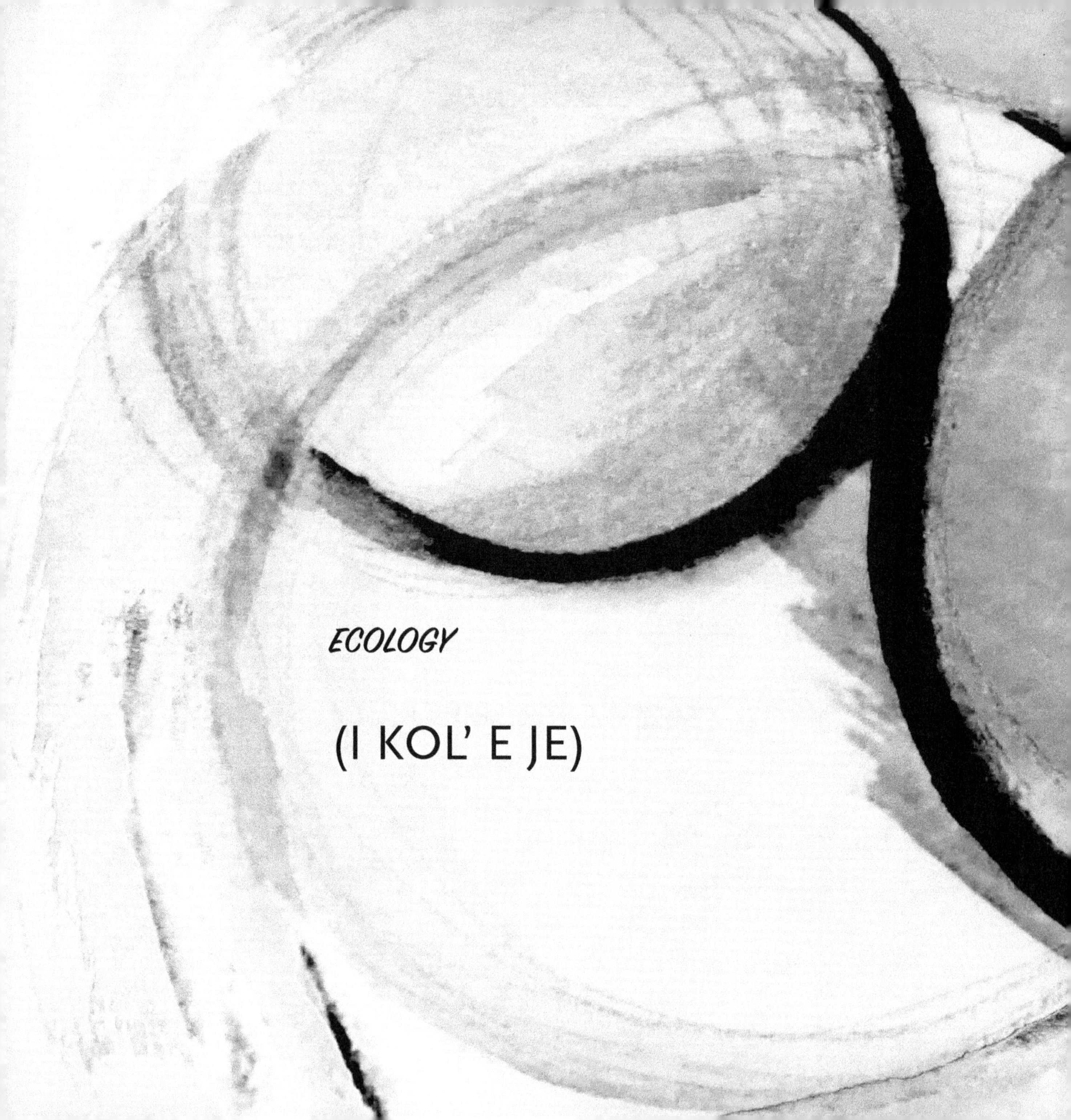

ECOLOGY

(I KOL' E JE)

A network of interactive and interrelated connections.

HOW DO YOU CONNECT WITH THE WORLD?

Relationships are connections with our world that open and draw out our potential. They beckon and engage us in new possibilities. They call us forward.

In this arrow write the ways you naturally move to meet the world. How do you interact with people? With nature? With your immediate surroundings? Are you interested in the details of the way something works or more broadly focused? Do you prefer to share in activities or in ideas? What are different ways you step into relationship with your world?

Our relationships also call us to listen, to hold another with respect, and to receive. They stretch us to deepen and widen the circle of our experience.

Think of times when you were open to listen deeply, times that created a wider field of connection for you. For example, have you ever heard someone's grievance and then made a change that shifted the relationship? Was there a time you took a walk and discovered an answer to a question? In this arrow note the situations and qualities that support you in listening.

Showing up is about interacting openly with the world around us. It is about contributing our particular gifts and skills in a way that honors another's gifts. Drawing upon the possibilities revealed through relationship, we develop ourSelves.

MAKE SPACE FOR THOSE THAT ANNOY YOU

We often want to turn away from the people or things that annoy or irritate us; they disrupt the shape of our lives. These are usually the people or situations that are not a natural "fit" for us in temperament or style or focus. But our lives are an ecosystem. In paying attention to the spaces we share through our relationships, we create the most potential for our own and others' joy.

I am reminded of a conversation with a friend who was struggling in a relationship. She shared her experience of making space for her partner in a way that allowed them both to be their better selves. *"I was feeling really frustrated and annoyed with my partner. I wanted more compassion. I was irritated because something I desired wasn't being offered. They were supposed to take care of it. Then I realized I needed to show compassion towards myself. I was looking outside for what I needed to give to mySelf. Finding that link to my annoyance helped me define a new space to work with the situation, shifting my attitude and their ability to respond."*

In paying attention to the spaces we share through our relationships, we create the most potential for our own and others' joy.

Discovery Practice: Imagine a situation when you have been annoyed with someone. Recall it in mind and heart. What do you notice in your body? Give your experience a shape and draw it in this space.

DRAW A SHAPE THAT REPRESENTS YOUR INITIAL EXPERIENCE OF THE ANNOYANCE.

Now relax and "soften" your annoyance. Hold the experience and listen. What are they trying to communicate? What thoughts float up in response? How does this insight change your experience? Draw a new shape to reflect any change.

HOW DOES THIS NEW INFORMATION INFLUENCE THE WAY YOU RELATE TO THIS PERSON?

WATER YOUR PARTNERSHIPS

Our relationships are shaped through an exchange of energy. They flourish when they are "watered" by our time, our attention, our goodwill and our willingness to learn. Attending to each other nourishes the environment in which we grow.

Not all the relationships that help us to thrive are human ones. My relationship with our family dog Gudrun is an example. She was good at partnering, giving generously of her time and attention. One evening when I was feeling particularly sad and alone, I sat outside on my deck. Gudrun purposefully came outside and joined me, sitting next to me without demanding anything. She just came and sat beside me. I felt deeply upheld in that moment by this very gentle act of friendship.

Another experience stands out as an example of Gudrun's good will. We were taking family pictures in the yard and in the hubbub of organizing the picture I had not thought to include her. But just before the picture was taken Gudrun came over without a fuss and posed with the group, very aware of including herself in the scene. I realized my oversight and her very gracious correction. Every time I walk by that family picture, I smile and am reminded of her spirited love. She widened my understanding of my connections with the world.

Discovery Practice: Choose a physical object, plant or pet that you care about. See it as a partner in your life.

Think about the conditions that help this partner to thrive. If it is a plant, what care keeps it healthy and flourishing? If it is an animal, when does it need your attention? If it is a car, what maintenance does it require to be in tip-top shape? Describe or draw these conditions in the first box.

Now, what are your needs in this relationship; how are you best supported? Create a picture of words or images in the second box that illustrates how you are served in the partnership.

Our relationships are fluid and responsive to the changing conditions in our lives. We must plant them in the soil of ongoing attention, shared joy and mutual respect in order for them to grow and develop in a lasting and sustainable way.

Discovery Practice: Spend some time thinking of your significant relationships and how you "water" them.

Write the name of one relationship in each of the four circles on the next page. Contemplating that relationship draw an arrow pointing toward the circle to identify the ways you "water" that relationship. For example, if it is a friend you might send them an unexpected card of appreciation.

Then draw another arrow pointing outward to name the ways they "water" you. Perhaps they take the time to attend a ceremony recognizing your community service.

Consider the many ways you may interact throughout a day or over time. What do you notice?

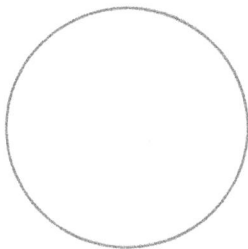

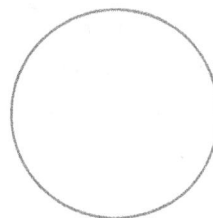

SHARE YOUR MISTAKES

I don't like making mistakes. I feel embarrassed, sure that I am alone in failing at a task and nervous about what someone else might think. My first response is to hide it away, to constrict. When I do, I sense that my "shape" pulls in and tightens. I feel isolated from my community and mySelf. In these moments of awkwardness, I am always grateful for those who offer understanding and empathy. Their connection helps me put my mistakes into perspective and brings me into a more resilient state.

One friend in particular comes to mind. She shapes a loving space of acceptance for herself and for others through her willingness to honestly meet a situation. She finds the humor in it and attends to the steps that will loosen the tension. Her example reinforces for me that making mistakes is a result of exploring the unknown and sharing mistakes acknowledges that we are all on a path of discovery.

Discovery Practice: Call to mind a time when you made a mistake. As you re-imagine the situation, what do you notice in your body? What happens to your breathing?

HOW WOULD YOU DESCRIBE YOUR SHAPE?

Now starting from this shape, consider a tiny change you can make that might alter your physical experience. Can you shift your breathing? Take a walk or move your body in some way? Smell a flower? Hug your pet? What other ideas come to mind?

Try out one of these changes and pay attention to what happens. Then try another. Keep making small changes until you come into a shape inside yourself that brings you a sense of ease. Illustrate your experience:

When you are finished take a breath. Center yourself with the standing practice on page 31 before moving on.

Resilience reflects our ability to return to a place of centeredness after a jarring or uncomfortable event. It is influenced by nurturing our sense of personal sovereignty through resources or qualities such as those we explored in the Self section. When we consciously attend to assets such as our own attitude and health, our work and creative expression, our community of friends and family, and our joys and our values, we have the resources to meet stressful events and maintain our internal balance. The more we strengthen the things that nourish and support us, the greater our resilience.

Reflection: Consider the resources available to you in your life.

Who are your supportive colleagues, good friends and family members?

What are your routines for sleep, exercise and rest?

Do you have an outlet for creative expression?

Do you feel financially stable and at ease in your surroundings?

Do you make time for play and being in nature?

From each of these five areas choose a resource and write it on one of the lines in the circle. Which are deep and strong? Which can use some tending?

Discovery Practice: Use this exercise to create an image that reflects the landscape of your resilience. How much of each resource is available to you right now? If an area offers only a small amount of energy and support, say you have not been sleeping well, put a dot on the line closer to the center of the circle. If it is an active asset for you, for example you have a strong exercise routine, then put your dot on the line toward the outer edge of the circle.

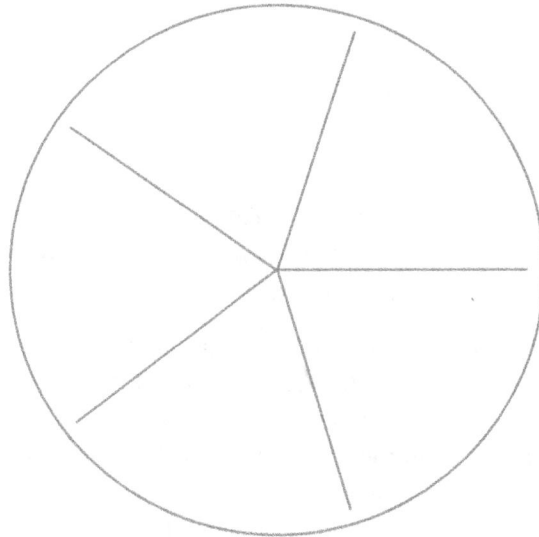

When you have marked all the lines, connect the dots clockwise. Shade in the area from the center of the circle to the edge of your outline. What shape do you notice? What does this tell you about the resources you have available? If you would like to call upon more resources in a particular area, what steps can you take? How can you bring more energy and attention to those areas?

TICKLE TABOOS

I use the idea of "tickle" as a metaphor for testing possibilities at the edge of things unexplored in my life. In this way "to tickle taboos" is to touch lightly and entertain the potential for a new opportunity. Working with what is true for me, I can move step by step to try out and perhaps welcome new and unexplored possibilities.

I have always admired those who can write. As a person whose natural expression is movement, putting my ideas into words feels awkward. I feel shy, exposed and vulnerable. Although I can happily write pages in a personal journal, to organize my thoughts in a public forum was challenging for me to consider. But my work required me to write a newsletter and make it interesting. I needed and wanted to tickle my taboos about writing. How to start? I challenged myself to consider the possibility of writing just one paragraph. Sometimes it took more than two days to write that paragraph, but with some encouraging feedback I persevered. After a year or so I noticed that the whole process had become easier.

Discovery Practice: Make a list of things you might want to explore but haven't because they seem outside the norms in your life. Notice what happens in your breath and your body as you write them down. Choose one of them. What small action would allow you to tickle the edge of that unfulfilled desire? Consider how you might put it into action.

As you imagine yourself doing it, notice how your body responds.

Write your observations here.

_____

_____

_____

_____

_____

_____

One way to open a relationship with something unexplored is to create a story around it. Our imagination can help us flirt with an idea and explore new relationships.

Discovery Practice: Take an activity from the previous page. Use the prompt, "What would it be like if?" to help yourself begin to imagine doing it. Explore the following questions to help you see how it might fit into your life.

Where do you do this activity? What are your surroundings?

Do you work with others? What people might you meet?

How does it feel in your life?

How else can you describe your new activity?

What small action could help you begin?

WHAT WOULD IT BE LIKE IF...

INTRODUCE YOUR CELL PHONE TO A TREE

I had an experience once while lying on a rock, basking in the sun. My feet were planted on the rock, knees up to the sky. I felt the sun on my face and I turned toward the warmth. For an instant, I felt planted like a flower, feet rooted in the earth, bloom reaching toward the sun. In that moment, I *was* a plant, rooted and growing.

Perhaps it is because of that experience that I love flowers and gardens. There is that little piece of shared awareness that links me with their life impulse, their joy. It lives in me as a connection to what it feels like to root and grow.

An instance of shared appreciation is also what one looks for when hoping to mediate a dispute between two parties, or when introducing one friend to another. Identifying a common experience helps us to establish a link.

As the creators of modern technology, we must help our tools find their place in the wider ecology of life. Creations such as a cell phone or the internet have become almost indispensable. This creates some tension, for though we get much inspiration from observing nature, we do not integrate our technologies back into it. However, as humans we have the capacity to take up this challenge. We can identify a common connection, even between a cell phone and a tree.

Reflection: Take your cell phone outside and place it under a tree. In your imagination introduce them to each other as if you are introducing two of your friends who do not know each other. "Cell phone, this is tree. A tree lives outside and sends its signal through its leaves, roots and fungi." "Tree, this is cell phone. It lives on a host without roots. It signals through electrical impulses in air and wire." Then just sit with your tree and cell phone and notice—without judgment—any thoughts that come up for you.

Discovery Practice: Any living thing is a part of a network of life through its flow of interaction and exchange. Pick a tree in your yard or neighborhood and identify its network below. Think of the elements it is made from, the systems that support its function—like the soil with its minerals and the sun with its energy. Also, who or what uses and benefits from its life? Examples might be the birds in their nests, or the kids with their treehouse. Write one of these elements next to each dot on the diagram:

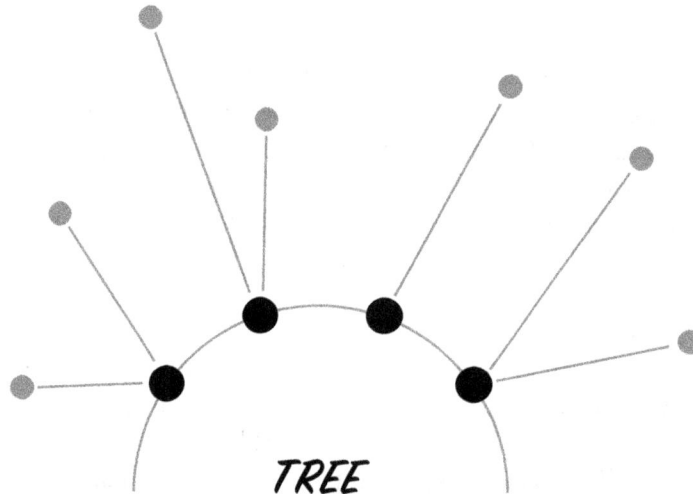

TREE

Now consider your cell phone and identify its network below. Think of the components that it is made from, the systems that support its function, like satellites and towers. Who or what uses and benefits from its existence in the world? Write one of these elements next to each dot on the diagram:

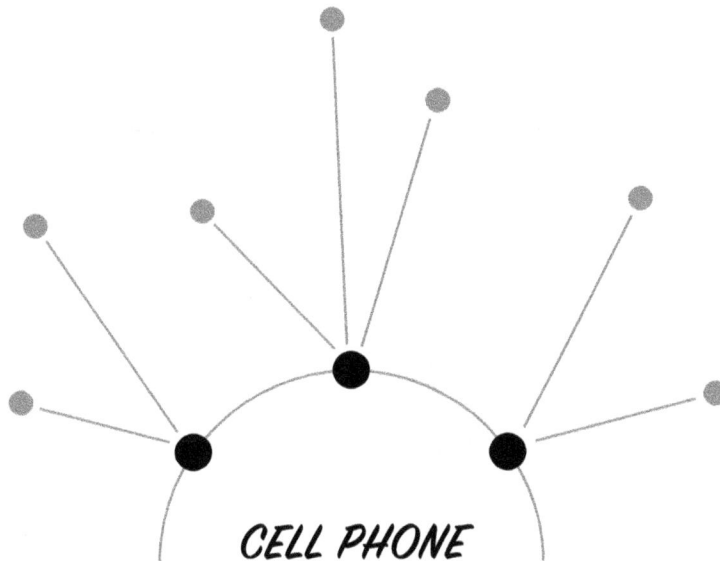

CELL PHONE

How do these two networks differ? What kind of connections do they share?

DESIGN FOR CONNECTION

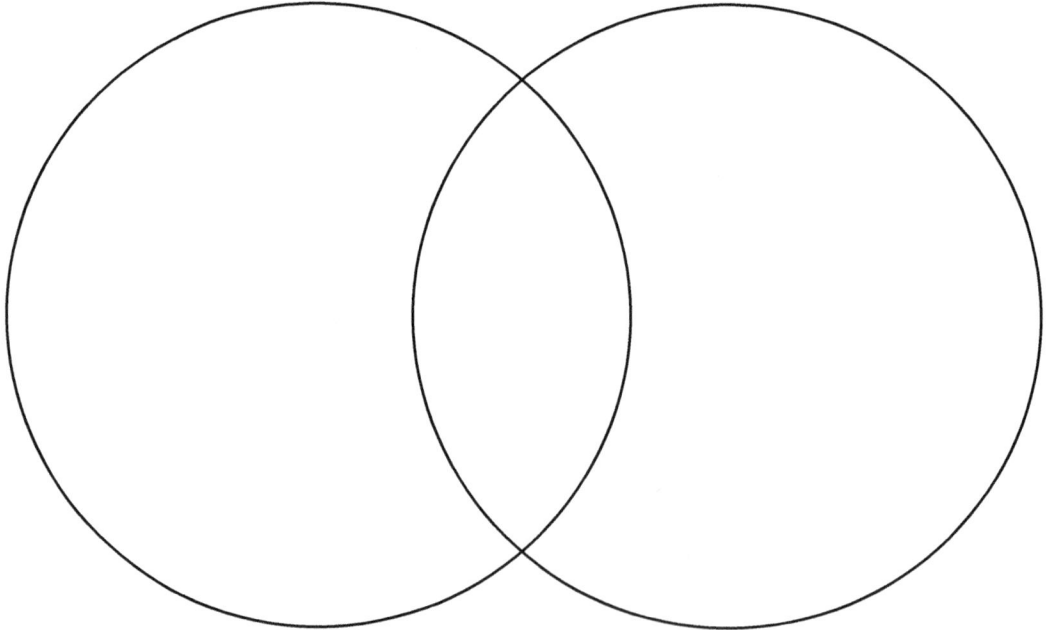

Let your ecology emerge from your place of truth, affirming its unique beauty and distinctness.

Reflection: Take your work with relationship a step further and imagine your life as an ecosystem. What kind of ecology are you? Are you a dense jungle or a spacious grassland? Brilliantly colored or softly muted?

Discovery Practice: Search for imagery that illustrates your ecosystem. Be open to the images that speak to you. Consider what juices your joy and opens up your gratitude from the exercises on pages 34-37 and 42-45. Remind yourself of what helps you to connect from pages 100-101. Where do you find them in this environment?

Arrange your images in the collage space on the next page.

Where do the elements of your life—family, friends, work, hobbies and passions show up?

Where is there space—openings where new information, people or activities can enter and be welcomed?

CREATE YOUR ECOLOGY COLLAGE:

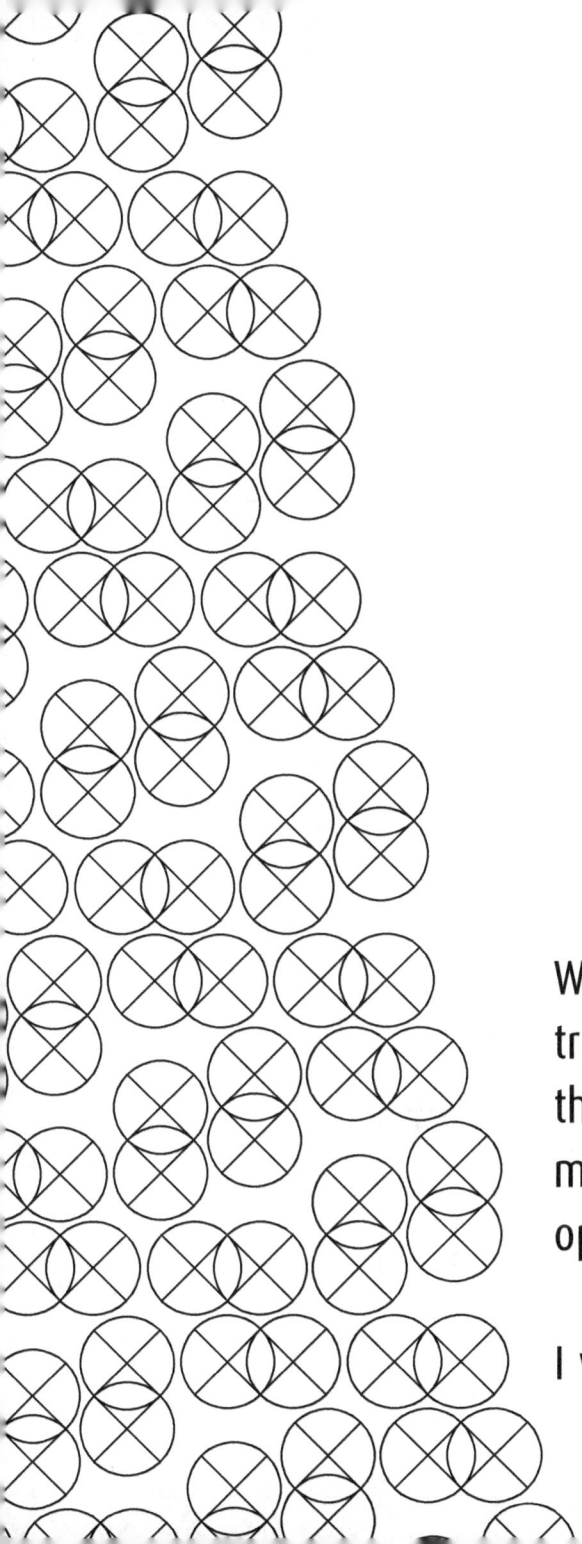

With attention and imagination,
trust and commitment, and
the ability to respond to
my connections, I meet my
opportunities.

I weave mySelf into the world.

CO-CREATION

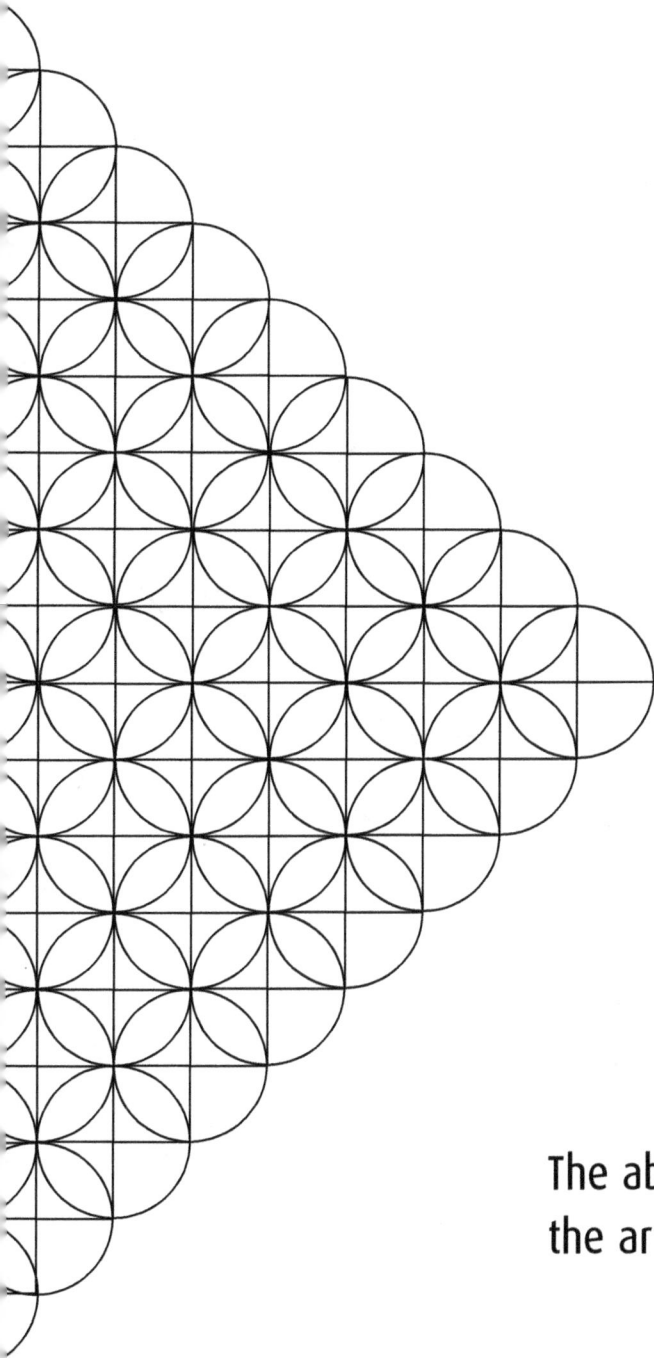

The ability to shape a space;
the art of inviting partnership.

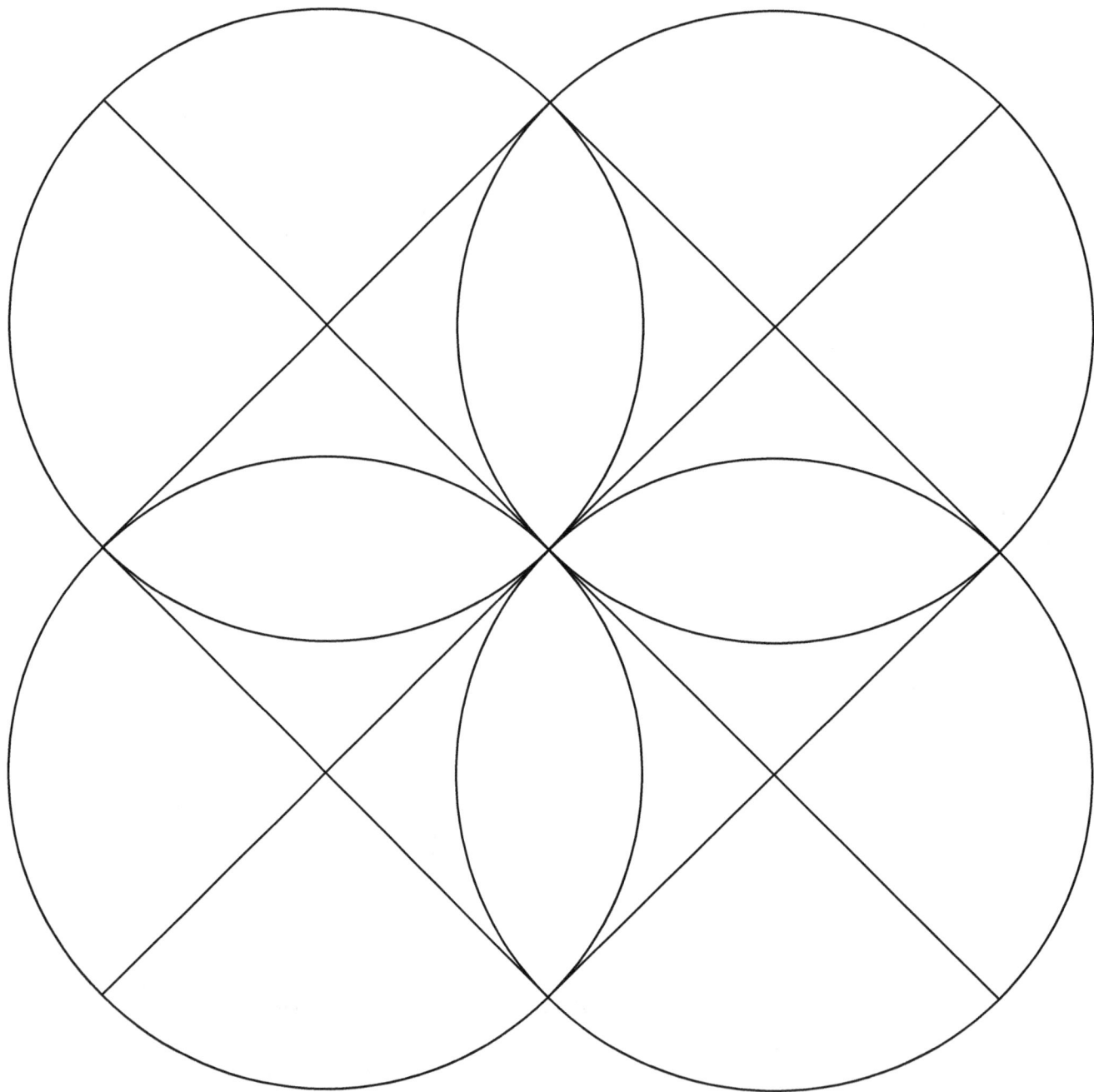

Gently cup your hands open in front of you. Turn one hand over and place it on top of the other.

WHAT DO YOU NOTICE?

WHAT DO YOUR HANDS FEEL LIKE TOGETHER?

WHAT SPACE DO THEY CREATE?

EMERGENCE

(I MUR' JENS)

The process of coming into existence,
the act of something new or hidden being revealed.

How do you invite partnership into your life?

Collaboration is an activity that shapes a space for something new to emerge. It offers the gift of transformation as well as the challenge of making space. Oxygen and hydrogen create water when they come together. When flour, milk and eggs mix, we have pancakes to eat. Each part adds their unique qualities but coming together they create a new wholeness— greater than the sum of its parts.

On this page name some of the things you have helped to create. For example, a project at work or a service to your community, a special dinner or a moment of new understanding.

Now consider what helped these activities or ideas to flourish and grow. What emotions and attitudes were present? What actions helped them unfold? How did others contribute?

Describe these conditions here.

Showing up is about shaping spaces of invitation. It is about opening space and making room for the unknown in our lives. Drawing upon our ability to collaborate, we invite the future to emerge.

FOSTER CONNECTION

We are more fully ourselves through our interactions with others and the world. Our network of connections forms an environment where we are stronger and possibilities can unfold. As we welcome partnership, we outline a space where the future can emerge.

umuntu ngumuntu ngabantu
(a person is a person through [other] persons)

Zulu saying

In improvisational theater, building a scene involves trust, cooperation and support. There is one particular improv exercise in which each actor specifically introduces their dialogue with the words, "Yes, and". To begin the scene a first actor steps up and establishes an activity and a role for themselves. The next actor comes in and says, "Yes" followed by "and...", affirming the activity of the scene and contributing to help define it further. Each time a person speaks, they begin their dialogue with "Yes, and" in this way continuing to develop the scene. "Yes" creates a space of affirmation and supports what has come before. "And" brings in a new element to enrich the scene's unfoldment.

Discovery Practice: In your conversations today begin your sentences with "Yes, and." Take the time to notice what is being said—"Yes"—and then consider how you might contribute—"and". Engage in a way that recognizes what is already in motion and then finds something to add which might help shape a next possible step.

You might notice you use "Yes, but" or even "No, but" when you speak.

DOES SAYING "YES, AND" MAKE A DIFFERENCE IN YOUR ATTITUDE OR IN SOMEONE ELSE'S RESPONSE? WHAT DO YOU NOTICE IN YOUR BODY'S RESPONSE?

Write your "Yes, and" statements on the next page with any responses you noticed.

YES,
AND......

WEAVE KINDNESS

When we weave fabric, we interlace different colored fibers in order to create a new piece of cloth. The strands are closely intertwined to create something new. When we weave kindness, we interlace our unique strands of Self and engage each other in relationship. Woven together in kindness we form the fabric of kinship.

Reflection: Think of a time someone was kind to you. What did it feel like, what part of your body responded? Now think of a time when you extended kindness to someone else. What did it feel like, what part of your body responded? How did that person respond to you?

Discovery Practice: Use the pattern below to identify some of the strands in your fabric of kinship. Next to each vertical line name an act of kindness you have offered. Next to each horizontal line, name an act of kindness you have received.

Kindness is different than being 'nice'. For me it includes respect and generosity; it upholds boundaries. Often it is an act of simply being present to another through the gift of our attention.

Discovery Practice: Begin by standing as you did in our very first exercise on page 31. Let your breath settle and find its rhythm, becoming steady and relaxed. Take a few minutes and tune in, become present to your relationship with yourself.

What is the kindest, gentlest choice you can make for yourSelf in this moment? Perhaps find a chair and sit down or go out for a run; in some way create a space of kindness for yourself.

How does that act of kindness land in your body? Are your shoulders soft or tense? What about your hips? Does kindness build a sense of kinship with your body? Write your discoveries here.

Now chose someone in your life—someone you interact with on a regular basis at home or work. Consider how you can weave a space of kindness and kinship with them today. What small act of respect, attention or generosity can you extend to them? What happens in your body when you do so?

How does this impact your perception of the other person? Write your discoveries here.

DOES YOUR KINDNESS BUILD A SPACE OF KINSHIP?

GIFT YOUR PASSION

To gift is to freely extend with the desire to enrich another. In gifting we share our abundance. There are so many different ways we give to those around us. The energies we project, the way we think, the looks we give and the words we use are all forms of sharing ourSelf. Each are opportunities to be generous and to invite others into a shared field of connection.

A friend once shared with me how hard it had been for her to socialize on the phone; she had dreaded returning a call, even to her friends. But she unexpectedly found a way to handle the situation. Once she had to return a call after participating in a yoga class and she noticed that it was easier to socialize during that exchange. To her surprise she realized that she felt totally relaxed, open and responsive. Now whenever possible she returns her phone calls after first attending to her physical well-being.

Reflection: When do you feel most "juicy", open and free to be generous with your energy whether physically, emotionally or mentally? Describe those times here.

_____

_____

_____

_____

_____

At the heart of passion is joy, the ability to stretch, to discover and to bring to life. When we gift our passion, we share with another what brings us alive and inspires us. One woman I know always brings flowers when she visits someone. She told me, *"I bring flowers because I love them. They inspire such delight in me. They bring me joy and I want to share that with others."*

Discovery Practice: Refer back to the Juice Up Your Joy exercises on pages 34-37. Reflect on one or two of your experiences. Attune to the sense of joy and lovingness that these memories draw out of you. You might imagine your heart overflowing with love or your spine glowing with love.

Feel your joy and love flow out from the core of your being down your arms and into your hands.

Reach out and touch an object. Imagine it accepting your overflowing love in its own way. Allow your energy to be available to this thing to brighten and nourish it.

As love flows out through your touch, it also flows in and circulates through your own being, bringing love to all parts of yourself just as you are bringing it to the item you are touching.

Touch as many objects as you wish.

WHEN YOU FEEL FINISHED, TAKE A MOMENT TO ALLOW THIS JOYFUL, LOVING ENERGY TO BE ABSORBED INTO ALL PARTS OF YOUR BODY.

ELECTRIFY HORIZONTAL SPIRITUALITY

Appreciation is like sunshine freely available to all; it has the power to warm us and draw us out. We empower and nourish something when we appreciate it.

David Spangler

To electrify something is to energize it, to connect it with a source of power. Most sources of power are measured in size and volume—solar power, hydro-electric power, fire-power, financial power. What we often forget is that we ourselves are also a potent source of power in the world. In addition to what we do, we carry and direct the energy of who we are through our loving attention and appreciation.

Reflection: Think of a time you felt appreciated. Notice the *felt sense* in your heart and mind and body. How did the power of appreciation impact you?

Now visualize or look at something or someone that you appreciate. Imagine them basking in your appreciation, free to absorb what you are offering.

What is the *felt sense* of this sharing?

What is its effect on you? We can't always know how the appreciation we offer is received, but we can notice how it impacts us.

Horizontal spirituality acknowledges sacredness as the common ground in which we are all rooted. My friend David Spangler beautifully illustrates this with a question about words written on a page:

LOOK AT THE TEXT ON THIS PAGE;

WHICH WORD IS CLOSER TO THE PAPER?

If we imagine the Sacred as a sheet of paper and the words written on it as life in its many expressions, then all life is in equal proximity to the Sacred. Though we may express it differently every being has equal access to sacredness.

When we pay attention to our friends, family and environment we can appreciate the unique spark of spirit that lives in each of them. Our attention and respect empower others as they unfold. With appreciation we energize the seeds of spirit everywhere around us.

Discovery Practice: Pay attention when you are participating in a conversation in your work or social environment. Notice how you are listening to each participant.

What factors influence your ability to appreciate the different voices in the conversation?

_____

_____

_____

_____

_____

_____

If you notice yourself tuning someone out—can you stop, maybe ask a question to discover something new that might help you appreciate them?

FALL INTO FREEDOM

I lived in The Findhorn Foundation community in my early twenties. Along with working in the kitchen, the garden and housekeeping, I was studying spiritual books, meditating in the sanctuary and trying to be more loving. But I found myself wanting to dance more than meditate, and swim in the sea more than sit in the library. One day I decided I needed to get more serious about my spiritual focus. So I created a plan for myself and tromped through my days very intent on clearing out my distracting habits at their root.

Several weeks later a friend invited me over for tea and asked what was wrong. She had noticed I wasn't my usual cheerful self. She listened to my story of clearing out my old habits and surprised me with her response. *"Instead of focusing on what you don't want to be,"* she said *"try using the metaphor of turning toward the sun. Put your attention on what you do want in your life."*

My friend's encouragement helped me lighten my self-criticism and opened a door I hadn't previously thought possible. Her advice to honor what was most true for me also opened spiritual doors. Love came much more easily as I put my attention and energy toward the activities that felt natural to me.

Discovery Practice: Consider a quality or condition that you would like to make more active in your life. What would it be like to pause, take a breath and turn to "face the sun"? What opens up when you turn your attention toward those qualities you want to strengthen?

Stay present to what is true for you. What are the natural ways you embody those qualities? Is there some slight shift of perspective that helps you discover a new possibility for yourself?

DRAW A SHAPE THAT REPRESENTS THIS EXPERIENCE FOR YOU.

Freedom comes with strengthening our "response-ability", with developing our skills to attend to what is ours to do. If we focus on freedom "from" something such as freedom from fear or freedom from restrictions, we are focusing on what we don't want. What would it be like to consider freedom "to" something, as in the freedom to act generously or the freedom to respond with honesty?

Discovery Practice: Is there a situation where you think, "I wish I had more freedom"? Notice your thoughts, are you focused on getting "freedom from" something? What small shift would open the possibility of "freedom to" in that situation? Put your shift into action. Does that small adjustment open new possibilities? Write your thoughts or experiences on the next page.

I WISH I HAD MORE FREEDOM TO....

DANCE WITH YOUR EDGE

Edges are not comfortable places; they feel a little risky—sometimes very risky. They are places of transition where differences meet. Edges are an interface of opportunity—a place where an exchange can happen.

At my edges I must be willing to take risks and let go of being in control in order to take advantage of opportunities. What helps me step forward and embrace my own edges is to think of dancing. Dancing engages me in a flow of relationship—with the room, with the music, with my partner and with other dancers. This flow helps me navigate through the uncertainty I experience at the edge of opportunity.

With practice edges can become like dancing partners. When we are responsive to their needs and responsible in maintaining our own balance we learn to engage them with lightness, grace and flexibility.

Reflection: Consider your work with the practices in this book. Pay close attention to what you discovered about your edges in the Edge and Relationship sections. What are the conditions that help you maintain balance in your life? How have you been learning to dance with your edge?

Write your responses here.

_____

_____

_____

_____

_____

_____

_____

Discovery Practice: Think of something new that you would like in your life. It might be an activity, a product, or maybe even a new habit. Think of it as a partner to dance with. Notice your body's response to this idea.

Now invite your partner to "dance" by setting aside time to try it out. How can you create a welcoming environment in order to interact with it? How do you take responsibility to maintain your balance in this relationship?

You want to have the freedom to move toward and step away. You want to be present to this partner and also to your own needs.

What is the quality or tempo of your engagement? Is it a waltz to get to know each other slowly? An intimate tango? A free-for-all mosh pit?

Check in with yourself as you follow through with this practice. What flexibility does this dance invite from you? How does this activity, product, or habit mesh with your life?

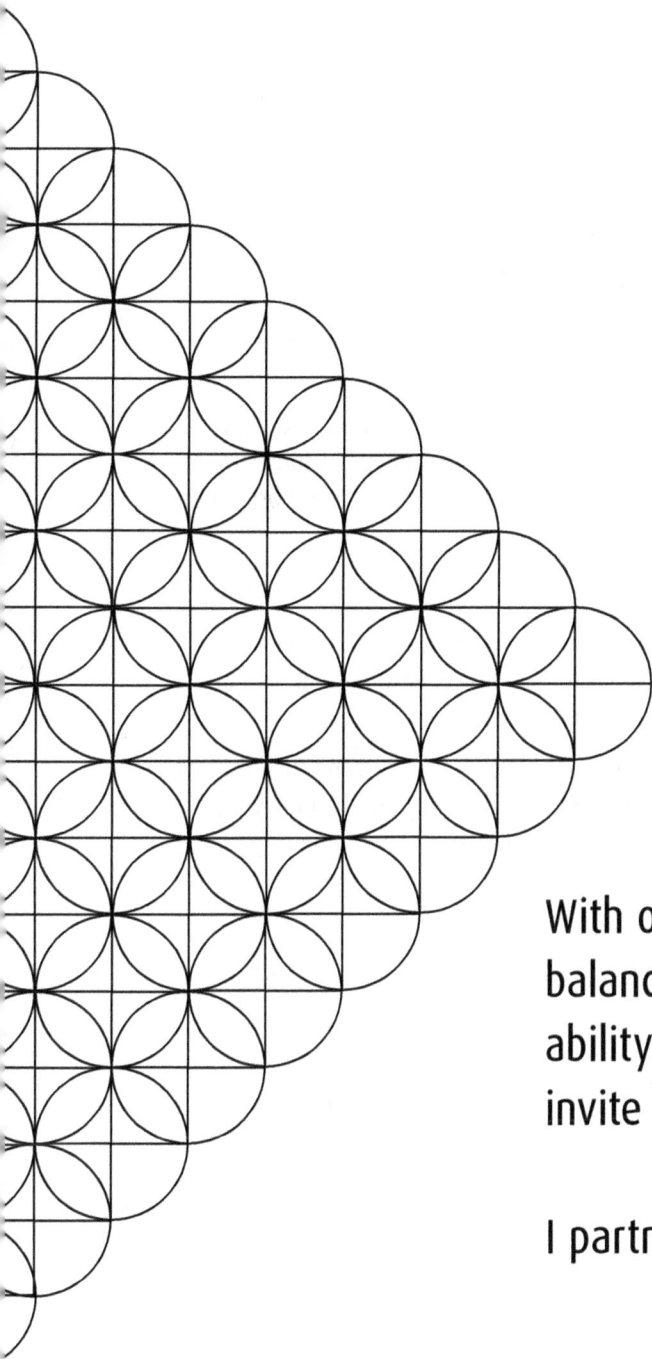

With openness and appreciation, balance and generosity and the ability to know the world as kin, I invite the future.

I partner my World.

SCULPT THE SACRED OUT OF YOUR DAY

The most available resource we have to create with is our own lives. We craft each day into its own painting, dance or song. Our daily actions may seem ordinary but they simply and naturally sculpt our lives into a work of art. With intention and attention, we bring our life-as-art into focus.

Discovery Practice: Set aside a small area in your home and place a few items there that connect you to treasured experiences and important moments of your life. What are the things that best represent what is most meaningful for you right now?

Let your space be true to your life experiences. Create a place where you can touch that which is unique and sacred to you. Use it to celebrate your experience of joy and beauty in the world or connect with courage in the face of adversity and loss. Let it be a touchstone of peace in the midst of change and upheaval. See it as a place where you *altar* your world.

Our choices matter, the things that delight us, the pain we experience and the connections we nourish sculpt our contribution to the aliveness of the world.

We are artists and our signature is vital.

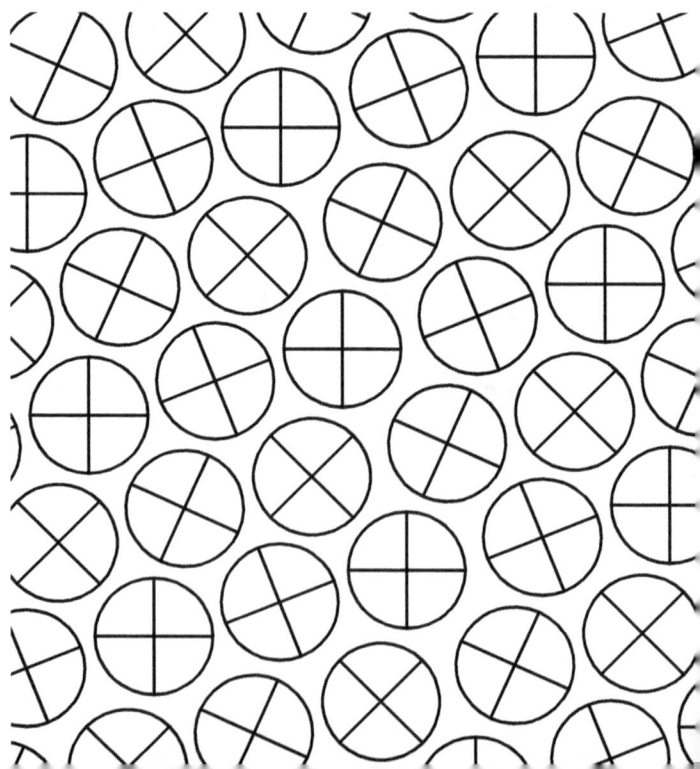

We are sovereign but not separate. With willingness, curiosity and a courageous heart we feel at home in the world.

We are not alone; we belong.

RESOURCES

Awakening the Creative Spirit by Christine Valters Painter and Betsey Beckman

Blessing: The Art and Practice by David Spangler

Come Closer by Dorothy Maclean

Focusing by Eugene Gendlin

Journey Into Fire by David Spangler

Kinship with all Life by J. Allen Boone

Kything: The Art of Spiritual Presence by Louis Savary and Patricia Berne

Manifestation: Creating the Life You Love by David Spangler

Non-Violent Communication by Marshall Rosenberg, PhD

The Call by David Spangler

The Hidden Life of Trees by Peter Wohllenben

The Power of Focusing by Anne Weiser Cornell, PhD

The Science of Parenting by Margo Sunderland

To Hear The Angels Sing by Dorothy Maclean

Yes, And: Lessons from The Second City by Kelly Leonard & Tom Yorton

Lorian Association - www.lorian.org

 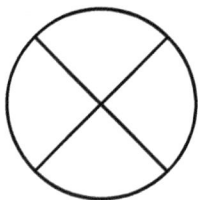  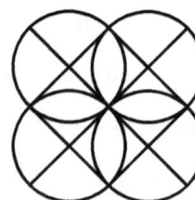

www.ingramcontent.com/pod-product-compliance
Lightning Source LLC
Chambersburg PA
CBHW080508110426
42742CB00017B/3036